Perspectives of Imperfection

towards stress free life

Dr. A. Robert Sam

INDIA • SINGAPORE • MALAYSIA

Copyright © Dr. A. Robert Sam 2024
All Rights Reserved.

ISBN
Paperback 979-8-89415-294-3
Hardcase 979-8-89415-387-2

This book has been published with all efforts taken to make the material error-free after the consent of the author. However, the author and the publisher do not assume and hereby disclaim any liability to any party for any loss, damage, or disruption caused by errors or omissions, whether such errors or omissions result from negligence, accident, or any other cause.

While every effort has been made to avoid any mistake or omission, this publication is being sold on the condition and understanding that neither the author nor the publishers or printers would be liable in any manner to any person by reason of any mistake or omission in this publication or for any action taken or omitted to be taken or advice rendered or accepted on the basis of this work. For any defect in printing or binding the publishers will be liable only to replace the defective copy by another copy of this work then available.

Contents

In Silent Conversation

Dear Readers!

The child, who thinks that the world is contained in the mother's womb, grows up, gets familiar with the outside world, lives in tandem with nature, and acquires intelligence. From childhood, till he attains old age, he meets with various situations and nurtures innumerable desires and dreams. With nature not restricting him to a certain way of life, he lives free every day of his life. He develops a desire to acquire wealth, property, position, intellect, life skills, and a deep attachment to The Almighty. He also comes to believe that happiness achieved, any which way, is life.

People are not able to achieve the success and benefits they hoped for, though they have nurtured such hopes while growing up. Instead, what they meet with are setbacks like failures, wrongs, ups and downs, anxieties, and yearnings. All these are seen as factors that determine the quality of one's life. No one can ignore these aspects of life. Our aim should be to demonstrate our ability to lead a wholesome life despite these stumbling blocks. There is an important reason why a man, considers these obstacles important, gets unduly stressed and spoils his life. It is because he tries to attain perfection or wholesomeness which is an attribute of God alone.

All those times, when man appropriates perfection as his own are the times mental stress manifests in his life. There is no age bar for this. This applies to all, from youngsters to the elders. The impact of this is different at different stages of man's life. People must be aware of how this difference occurs. What is the connection between mental stress and perfection at various stages of our lives? How does one deal with mental stress in those circumstances? How can one confront such stress? How can a person manage such mental stress? This book explains the ways and means, through real-life incidents, to find solutions to these questions.

The different life contexts and the mental stress associated with them are compiled and presented, altogether in this single book. This will help every reader not only to understand the nature of one's mental stress but also the nature of mental stress at other stages of life and thus pave the way for them to be prepared. By understanding the previous situations and with the present explained, he will be able to set right his future. Life begins with one being completely unaware of things, to a stage when you begin to understand them but are unable to experience them. You then move on to the final stage when you have fully understood them, but by then you are no longer alive to experience them. Therefore, if this realization or understanding happens at the beginning itself, life will become meaningful and with this aim in mind, this book has been written, for all ages, from the young to the old.

In Silent Conversation

This book highlights the fundamentals of life and the importance of imperfection for a stress-free life. Parts of the book will focus on lessons that will make you understand life situations, some will force you to think and some motivate you to act. The writer intends to make you realize, think, and act according to the context and according to the circumstances.

Why mental stress? Why perfection? Let us uproot these from our lives. Let us satisfy the necessities of life. Let us fulfill our commitments. Our life is in our hands; let us live up to it.

Thanks!!

1

Introduction

Walking has become a popular choice of exercise for people of all ages. They take to this with enthusiasm since it benefits their physical well-being. This trend can be attributed to the increasing awareness about the impact of various strange diseases, discovered and undiscovered, and the ways and means to combat these diseases. Besides, the correlation between walking and good health has been clinically demonstrated.

It is a well-known truth that the root cause of various kinds of diseases is digestion and blood circulation. Apart from this, one has to maintain mental health for a disease-free life. People undertake walking as an exercise to maintain both mental and physical health. They also go in for a few simple exercises like cycling, yoga, skating, jogging, skipping, dancing, and swimming.

To understand things better, I decided to ask them why they do these physical exercises without fail. I thought, as detailed above, the answer would be 'for digestion and good blood circulation'.

I did not get the answer I had expected. Instead, apart from a few, a larger percentage of people said, 'to reduce mental stress and to maintain good health'. This made me think and consider their answer from different angles. What is the correlation between these exercises and mental stress? What is the medical explanation for mental stress? Where does it originate from? How does it originate? How does its impact differ as per a man's status or condition? What are the ways to reduce mental stress? This book has been written to find answers to these questions and the connection between mental stress and the life of man under various situations.

Whether it is physical exercise or walking, the one thing that is experienced in both is bodily fatigue. In spite of knowing this, why do people invite such fatigue every day? The world has understood that there is no gain without pain. This principle has been followed by people from time immemorial. But this has been losing its significance over time. These days, people do not hear about or see the benefits of hard work and the resultant fatigue as life has become digitized and machine-driven. Instead, a different kind of fatigue is gaining currency due to lifestyle changes and that is mental fatigue. This is worse than bodily fatigue.

Mental fatigue is the first sign/manifestation of mental stress. To get rid of this fatigue one takes up physical exercises. Why does one invite physical fatigue by undertaking physical exercises to rid oneself of mental fatigue? Is that the best way? If not, what are the other ways? Based on the inputs given by those who have taken up physical exercises, this book answers the questions. People bear any amount of body pain and agony along with physical pain. To get rid of the mental fatigue people are ready to spend even their precious/valuable time. How has this acquired so much importance that the whole world is engaged in this struggle to get rid of mental fatigue along with mental stress?

Perspectives of Imperfection

Measurement is one of the most necessary things to evaluate any object in the world or to impose an action. Based on measurement, one can measure the action. One can also express it. In this instance, physical fatigue is measured through physical pain. At the same time, how does one measure mental fatigue or mental pain? How to control it without a measuring scale? All these are questions that crop up in people's minds.

The physical fatigue that can be measured makes one's life better. The mental fatigue that cannot be measured spoils his life. It is our paramount duty to find out what is necessary to better our lives. Is physical fatigue important? Is mental stress important? How and from where does the mental stress that spoils a man's life make its appearance? We can attribute quite a few reasons for this.

Is it because of one's poverty? No.

Is it because of a lack of facilities? No.

Is it because of ill health? No.

Is it because of excess wealth? No.

Man has six senses which is what makes him different from all other forms of life. Man, even with his six senses, cannot escape mental stress. Animals too have mental stress but its impact is seen very less on them. But the man with his six senses is indeed responsible for the mental stress on the animals.

On examination, it becomes clear that the cause of stress is the failure to know the three things of place, object, and time, and to use one's knowledge in a proper perspective. Depending on the time, place, and object, the action that man undertakes is called 'his attitude' and it is then that his actions become the cause for his mental stress. The desire for wholesomeness or perfection is the reason that brings about changes in a man's attitude, and this creates mental stress in him. It is his practice to change his lifestyle, in his quest for perfection. What is its effect?

Is man able to live a meaningful life as per his plan? Is he able to achieve his life's ambition that easily? Yes is a very rare answer to these questions. The reason for this is man's eternal search for perfection and hence let us own and accept 'Imperfection' instead of 'Perfection'. Let us learn through this book how we can lead a happy life, by giving importance to imperfection and thus avoiding mental stress at every stage of life.

Man has, since time immemorial, had the habit of comparing himself to others and his possessions with those of others. His sense of satisfaction or dissatisfaction is a result of the information that he acquires about this. Whatever the result, he will not give up on comparisons. He makes these comparisons at every stage of his life. The question as to why he does it needs a moment's consideration. He not only makes comparisons, but he also brings his need for perfection into this and changes his lifestyle accordingly.

Perfection is an endless quest. Are people able to say 'yes, this is the definition of perfection'? No. In the name of perfection, people go in for physical changes/ plastic surgery to look better and for self-defense. Not in these physical adjustments alone, but they also make comparisons in actions and skills in performance to attain perfection. They make changes to their throat to enhance their voice quality. They continue to make various other changes in their lives. To attain this elusive perfection, they continue this struggle till the end of their lives. What could be the result of this struggle for man?

Based on his intelligence, he defines certain as perfection, and towards that, he strives to find not only progress in every instance and every action but also seeks success, appreciation, and validation for that. He gets pleasure and satisfaction, even if temporarily. Even then, his race towards perfection does not end because the goalpost for perfection, its position and definition keeps changing as per their perception and their intelligence. As the position of perfection as a goal keeps changing, this struggle continues. It does not end here. He does not stop at comparing himself; he expects perfection in every product of his creative skills and perfection in his skill of doing the work.

Thus, from changing his physical appearance to his skill in doing things, to the products of his creative skill, and the art of creation, he compares them with others, based on his thinking skills, and attains satisfaction. As days go by, and as the circle of his genius widens, the comparisons also grow wider and wider until they encompass the whole world. At this level he encounters failure. Unable to accept this, he is completely disheartened. What could be the reason for this? It should not be forgotten that perfection is defined, at the global level, by people who are imperfect.

Just as man expects perfection in doing, the method of doing, and the skill of doing, he also expects this perfection from other fellow humans. What happens when parents expect perfection from the children, husband and wife from each other, the teacher from his students, and leaders from their workers? In the respective circles, these expectations give rise to mental strain and stress.

When we compare ourselves with others, we can see two different kinds of people - one who has struggled all through life, worked tirelessly, and continues to work hard, and the other, who lives on the proceeds of the group who worked themselves to the bone. Both of them have mental stress. The ones who reap the benefits of the hard work of others are found to be under more mental stress than those who have toiled hard. The reason is that the mental relief realized through hard physical labor is not available to them.

Even the distinguished and noble men of the world will have their sagas of mental stress. They would have become achievers having struggled with mental stress and strain. Of course, there are a few who have not been able to/ counter their mental stress and then there are those who progress through it. Why is it that the one who has progressed at the global level and has secured global recognition and appreciation is unable to overcome his mental stress? The reason, one should not forget, is that it is the people themselves who are responsible for such mental stress. This situation arises only when we give importance to the decisions of others over our own or when we subject ourselves to be affected by their ridicule. The first and foremost way of combating this would be to have confidence in ourselves and our possessions. We should understand that we alone are responsible for our successes and our failures.

Will only perfection help us enjoy life? No. will only imperfection be of use, is the question that this book aims to analyze. The author's design is to establish a communion of all minds, to urge them to read from the beginning to the end of this book that describes how to deal with the nuances of every situation in life and act accordingly.

Do read !! Do benefit from it !!

2

The Role of Perfection in Our Lives

Perfection is one characteristic of human life that is expected in various situations. This demand for perfection in all circumstances be it at the office, festivities, schools and colleges, investigative agencies, family, married life, gatherings of relatives and friends, is a cause of great stress. Stress builds gradually and is a weapon that sharpens itself through the passage of months and years as it wreaks havoc on the mind bit by bit. Stress works insidiously and covertly. In other words, one does not know how and when it will affect us. It is a slow, silent killer with almost no symptoms visible externally. Let us examine a few instances to understand how stress affects us in our daily lives.

Perfection in the Workplace

An office is a place where one works with one's superiors and colleagues, and where one spends a greater percentage of life. Take the case of an employer and employee. If either were to seek perfection in every aspect of their work life, consequences would certainly be unexpected. We should remember that the focus in this instance is on the attitude of the employer and employee.

Two employees were tasked with similar projects. There were two ways in which the completed task could be submitted. One employee could've turned in his work to his boss saying, "Sir, I have completed the task to my satisfaction. If, however, there are improvements and changes to be made I will happily make them with your guidance". The other employee could've submitted his work saying, "I have completed the task. I have ironed out all the wrinkles and assure you that no errors can be found". Both ways of submission are normal. That such a simple situation could draw forth such consequences is certainly surprising.

We can learn a few truths from this incident. Look closely at the reaction of the employer. Compare it with an event in your life. The employer's attitude is evinced through his actions. The employer would look the first employee in the eye, and appreciate him for his effort. He would feel a rush of camaraderie towards the first employee. In the interaction with the second employee, if one observed closely, the boss would not meet his employee's eyes. His attention would turn inwards and as he pretends to scan the document he would allow his mind to wander and dismiss the employee with just an "Okay".

Why this difference in treatment? Both employees had completed the task satisfactorily. However, the manner in which the work was submitted also influenced the boss's response. The quality of the completed task was not the only factor in judging an employee's capability. The employer's caliber, world view and motivations work together to influence his reaction.

What is our takeaway from this? It is natural that a person will receive such a response whenever he assumes that his work is complete and claims that it is perfectly done. This, however, is only a simple example. This does not end here. What next then? Unwittingly, the employer, when discussing this incident with his colleagues or friends, would pass judgment on not just the claim but the person who made the claim. This inevitably would lead to conveying the wrong impression about the employee to others. Such a situation would cause a lot of unhappiness in the workplace, making it an unpleasant experience, the effect of which will be long-lasting. This negative experience will be carried over into their personal lives too. This is the undeniable truth of every workplace. This is not something observed, nor is it something that can be expressed aloud. This unhappiness is repressed in the mind and slowly but surely begins to affect the person physically making him ill. The result of this invariably is mental stress.

All employees, without exception, are subject to this kind of stress either directly or indirectly in their workday lives. Such stress is inevitable. This is not a reflection of their skill at work at all. One can be subject to stress even while doing nothing. People who dedicate themselves completely to their work too experience stress. One needs to accept the truth that stress is inescapable and find a way to deal with it. When considered in terms of world mental health statistics the percentage of people suffering from mental stress is greater than those who do not.

The world is amazed that stress is the root cause of many diseases affecting both young and old. In order to deal with this, people engage in fancy hobbies like aerobics, pilates, yoga, and other physical activities. These, however, provide only temporary relief. What is one to do? First, one cannot break away from relationships either at home or at work. One has to move on in life. Second, the initial steps towards dealing with stress are dealt with in this book. One can choose from a variety of tools suggested in the latter part of the book to cope with various situations, to become stress-free, and to gain the ability to deal with crises with sangfroid. The best way to deal with stress at home or work is to develop a flexible attitude in one's personality.

The Role of Perfection in Festivities

Festivities are occasions where there is a meeting of minds, an interchange of pleasantries and well-being, an exchange of views, and welcoming of the guests even as the rituals go on. Each one present is bound to be of a different mindset. It is only natural for the organizer to be anxious before the event hoping that things go as planned and speculating if they indeed did, after the event. This, of course, is dependent on one's resources and the attitude of the invitees. Let us examine this with an example.

Parents expect the planned event will take place perfectly as envisaged, be it a celebration of the birth of a child, a birthday, or a wedding. They would want to follow traditions and look for an auspicious day to celebrate. They would pay particular attention to keeping ready the things needed for the occasion, like the festive clothing, the toys, the cleanliness and hygiene to be maintained on that day. They would plan in great detail the order of ceremonies and social etiquette to be followed on that day, in their attempt to be completely and perfectly prepared. But then, whatever the occasion it is not possible to be sanguine and believe that things have happened as planned or to be able to exhibit to others that indeed this was how it was planned and carried out.

On such occasions, he will make it a point to invite his neighbors, colleagues, family, and friends to the birthday or wedding and ask for feedback from them. Unexpectedly, he receives many compliments regarding the conduct of the event. Everybody compliments the hosts. When face to face with the host, the invitees - friends, criticizers, faultfinders, and enemies too, will heap praises. The event organizer will be drenched in a shower of compliments pouring on him. But what about his mental state at the end of the day?

After accepting the good wishes and seeing off the guests, he will be assailed by a small doubt. Did I organize the event perfectly? were the compliments sincere and honest? Or were the guests just being polite? Needing reassurance he then sits down to have a free and frank discussion with the family about the feedback. After analyzing the feedback, he comes to the conclusion that whatever anyone may say, he has done his best. He reassures himself that given the resources at his command, this was the most he could have done under the circumstances and gets back to the routine of his life. This attitude, of course, is the only way forward if one wants to lead a life free of tension and stress.

Unable to convince himself that he has a perfect plan for the festivity, be it a birthday or a wedding, he seeks validation from relatives and neighbors, friends, and colleagues through their feedback. Rather unexpectedly, he gets positive feedback. He gets such responses even from those who normally crib and find fault with everything when asked for their feedback face to face. How can it be otherwise? But then, after all is done and dusted, he begins to question himself- did I do such a good job, or is it all an attempt to make me feel good? In any case, he goes through the whole proceedings threadbare with his family with a long and frank discussion wherein everyone puts forth their takeaways. Finally, he concludes that he has done his best with the resources and support at his command and decides to move on with his life.

But then, does one come to terms with oneself as would be the ideal case? He harbors negative feelings and stress within him. When he accepts an invite from a friend or relative and attends the function, he cannot but compare and contrast the present occasion with the function he had recently organized. He does not hesitate to point out the shortcomings openly, much to the discomfiture of the friend or the relative, and beats his drum about how well his family function was carried out.

And in case that occasion turns out to be grander and better organized than his own, he leaves it midway without partaking of the festivities and returns home disappointed. He is now convinced that his family function was not such a roaring success after all. His mindset is thus determined by the comparative success or grandeur of the functions he then attends. This continues with every function he participates in and results in harboring negative feelings within himself.

The takeaway from the above example is that one should not expect completion or perfection in life, I have to lead my life as best as I can depending on my caliber and my circumstances. One should live by the principle that this is the best I can do given my situation, my resources, and the support at my command. My satisfaction that I have done my best is paramount. I cannot dance to others' tunes or to try to satisfy others. It is this absence of perfection and completion that lends meaning and purpose to my life. It is this lack of perfection that goads me to better myself. Only He is perfect. Only what He creates is perfect. Only what He does is perfect. Man fails if he tries to emulate his Creator.

The Role of Perfection in Schools and Colleges

Let us now take a look at the interplay of the role of perfection in the life of school-going children. Here too, we see the effect of mental stress on children as they seek to be perfect in their work. School-going children come from varied family backgrounds. The standard of education, the opportunities, the financial resources and the circumstances under which their parents pursued their education are vastly different from those of their children. Many students put up a brave front to obviate the strained family circumstances of their fellow students. There are many students with the desire to succeed in spite of their financial constraints, with grit, determination, and self-confidence. Even though the uniform expresses unity, many people can be seen to be offended by incidents that go wrong.

Take a classroom situation. What happens when the teacher praises a student, not only for his neat appearance but also for his academic excellence, and presents him as a role model for the entire class? Each child in the class comes with emotional baggage. They are aware of their family background, their limitations, and both the financial and social status of their parents. They also have a fair idea about their teachers. When a particular child becomes the object of praise openly in the class, it could have a salutary effect on some who feel encouraged and wish to emulate the topper, while some may even resent this and develop an inferiority complex. It cannot be said that the child so praised remains unaffected. He may even lose the friendship of some of his classmates, leading to his feeling isolated from others.

The teachers, in most cases, do not take into consideration the effect such praise may have on the minds of his less-endowed classmates. Does it lead to enhanced performance in other students in the class? If the teacher can highlight the hard work of the child and the progress in his academic performance, it could have a laudatory effect on the others in the class. The only gold standard to be considered here is the amount of hard work, persistence, and consistency of the child and not one's wealth, family status, power, or influence. Keeping this in mind let us strive for success, not giving in to developing an inferiority complex but power ahead with self-confidence. Let us scale the heights of success, overcome the differences the society thrusts upon us, and become role models for others.

Perfection or completion is not wearing expensive clothes, scoring a perfect grade in all subjects, and not even being regular to school throughout the year. Perfection is when he can apply the knowledge gained during his academic pursuit to real-life situations, thereby keeping in step with his fellow schoolmates, the society, and the community in which he lives. Perfection is when he understands the meaning of life. Perfection is when he progresses in life in sync with his fellow humans. Such a person is considered the ideal, worth emulating, or a role model for society. But, such an ideal person should not take it upon himself to be the only ideal to be followed by others in society. This idea of perfection, though attributed to him, should not be taken for granted by him. He will be able to live up to this ideal only when he comes to terms with his weaknesses, too. For society to accept him, he should be able to lead a life that will be beneficial to himself and the society at large and together they can proceed on the road to further progress and improvement.

The Role of Perfection in the Depth of Hygiene and Sanitation

Perfection and imperfection are two sides of the same coin. When one looks for perfection it means he is trying to rise above his imperfections. There is a tendency to dismiss as 'imperfect' the situation from which he is trying to raise himself in his struggle for perfection.

Take the case of those engaged in cleaning and sanitation work, be it at home or in public spaces daily. Once the cleaning is done, the garbage thus collected is disposed of in bins for transportation to landfills or for segregation. Homes and streets are completely clean.

Is that the real situation? One area is cleaned, but the cleaners have to deal with uncleanliness in another part of the city. The garbage dumps are thoroughly unclean. The cleaning, collecting, and disposing of the accumulated garbage is an ongoing process. To attain perfection in the process of cleanliness, one has to go past the imperfect state of uncleanliness. Here, we can observe two processes at work. One is the state of cleanliness, and the other is the struggle for cleanliness. Instead of appreciating the cleaning of individual households as perfect, it is far better to label as perfect the labor of sanitation workers. Theirs is the labor that is done in service of the nation.

It is an inescapable fact of life that there can be no cleanliness without uncleanliness. Even the person who is a stickler for health and hygiene might sometimes find himself in situations where he has to let go of his scruples. This happens invariably when one has to travel long distances. He may face situations where he may be forced to use unclean restrooms for his morning routines. Consider his situation. What is he to do then? These situations arise especially when he is traveling by bus. Some restrooms available on the way may be the very epitome of cleanliness and hygiene. It may be decorated with colorful and fancy lights. In such an environment, one becomes unable to fulfill even his urgent needs. He would begin to look for a less fancy, less clean, but more convenient and private place. He will feel truly relieved only after this. I believe this to be true. In urban areas, some dirty hidden places become wonderful places to benefit the needy, big and small, men and women, poor and rich.

There are times in one's life when one is forced to forego preconceived notions of cleanliness and look for alternatives that may not necessarily conform to normal standards of hygiene. Everyone, irrespective of their age, gender, or financial status, without exception, has faced such situations, at some time or the other in their lives. They may not openly admit this, fearing that their so-called veneer of perfection may be found out. In the same manner, some among us would rather stick to our false notion of being perfect and put up with extreme discomfort and suffer silently even at the risk of bodily harm to oneself.

In fact, it is these unhygienic surroundings that give scope for a lot of scientific research in areas of health and hygiene. It is worth remembering that the need for perfection or hygiene is felt precisely because of these unhygienic surroundings. It becomes imperative to appreciate those who tirelessly strive to keep our surroundings clean instead of just wishful thinking for clean and safe surroundings. Do not forget to thank those sanitation workers who keep the public places clean. This acceptance of the importance of these workers will help rid oneself of the feeling of superiority and help us realize that we are all equal.

The Role of Perfection in Married Life

In the case of married life, the concept of wholesomeness or perfection is not dependent on any one of the partners. A marriage is an amalgamation that unites both the husband and the wife in their entirety. This intervention indeed happens from two different angles, but it is in the context of marriage that the role of wholesomeness or perfection is at a premium. The husband and the wife come from different backgrounds, and they are untired in this bond of marriage subject to societal, caste, and religious precepts, canons, and dictates. They come from different cultural backgrounds, with different mindsets, different traits, and attitudes. These differences bring about a turning point in the initial stages of their married life. Simultaneously it brings along with it stress and pressures to conform to two different traditions of the communities they belong to, the religious rituals, practiced in their respective families, different societal constraints or restrictions, expectations from two different communities, and also to their normal actions/practices. Under such circumstances, they are unable to lead a life of their choice, having to compromise/accommodate the advice from their families and relatives and the expectations of their communities.

The marriage will find itself in troubled water if the wife and/or the husband were to steer the ship of their marriage in different directions based on the wisdom and advice they receive from their respective environs. Huge waves, violent storms, whirlpools, and nature's unexpected wrath in the form of sudden severe hurricanes, massive icebergs in certain spots, and sometimes just the frozen snow, are all part and parcel of life that could rock the marriage boat. As long as there is water in the ocean, the above struggle of life will continue. The struggles faced by the ship called life, like the waves of the sea, never cease.

Under the circumstances, vehement arguments, differences of opinion, mutual resentment, and despair are inevitable in one's wedded bliss in the early stages of marriage. This happens in everyone's life. No one can predict when it will end. Understanding each other can take days, months, and years. As already mentioned, the problems begin when the two are compared to each other. It gets stronger and compares the two families and what belongs to the families and eventually creates divisions. Why is this?

The skill sets of the husband and the wife, as well as the status of their respective families are bound to be different. For their

   Perspectives of Imperfection

marriage to work and to be able to lead a peaceful and conflict-free life together, what is paramount is how these differences are resolved. One may be very efficient or very incompetent. It is how one addresses these perceived differences in each others' status, financial and/or cultural, and their life skills and aptitudes that will determine how well they can lead a normal, stress-free life as a couple.

They may be highly skilled in their fields before marriage. It is only natural that they try to exhibit their skills after marriage. The husband may be willing to help others. He may be good at drawing, painting, or gardening, to name a few as may the wife be at painting, knitting, embroidery, artwork, etc. Lending a generous helping hand to get the work done is the norm in any family so that the work gets done, quickly and efficiently. This effective and successful competition of the work happens because one of the two is more skilled than the other. But what happens in such cases? Are both their contributions recognized and appreciated as being of the same standard? Since there is this stark difference in recognition received for their work at every stage in life, it makes way for mental stress to make its formal entry into their married life.

All of us are ready to lend a helping hand to those in need. Though this is to be appreciated, what needs to be considered is whether your help is accepted wholeheartedly. If that is so, then one can go ahead and extend all help needed. But the mistake we make is to leave it at that. They may not like the people they are helping to be proud or others to be proud of them. This should be observed closely. If any reluctance appears, taking it into account and making a decision early on will pay off. Also, the helper may not only think in his heart that I have done my duty, but may not show any pride. This is a great way. How do we know that the help you give is needed? Let us look at a real-life situation for comparison.

You have helped someone and you share this with your friends or your relatives, expecting appreciation. Consider carefully if your act of extending a helping hand to this person is being acknowledged. If not then what do you need to do under similar circumstances, when you want to help someone, point out a third person and leave it at that.You can tell the person who has approached you for help that you will get the work done through this third person and get the work done by yourself, i.e. by the husband without the wife knowing about it or by the wife without the husband's knowledge. This way both their egos are not hurt. You need not make a show of your having helped someone in need since the very act of helping instills positivity in you and thereby lessens any possible mental stress. The reason for including a third person in this situation is to avoid a clash of egos between a husband and wife. Thus, the relationship between them will be very good.

As against this let us look at a situation where things happen in the background.

The phrase 'Lucky guy' or 'Lucky girl ' is often heard in conversations among friends or relatives, especially in long conversations. When a woman is patted on the back and called a lucky girl, she might feel elated at the compliment. But do consider for a moment if it is not a backhanded compliment. This phrase could be used in any of the following scenarios.

The person so addressed could be weak in his/ her ability to carry out daily activities and maybe it is the husband or the wife who steps in to fill the lacuna.

Or it could be either the husband or the wife who heaps enormous praise for the work done by the other.

Or it could be a third person who does not point out the faults evident in the work done.

It could be someone who leads a simple life, having sacrificed all pleasures for the sake of his/ her partner and opting for a life of hard work.

Or it could be a husband who realizes that his wife is rather delicate and so chooses to do all the work by himself without subjecting his wife to any kind of hard work.

It is obvious that this is invariably the case in most situations wherein we find a person in the background who is ready to fill in for the other partner in a marriage. Under such circumstances, when the wife is told that she is a lucky girl, is the praise for the husband or the wife? It is certainly a praise for the husband but he is not the recipient of the praise, his wife is. This should make the wife wonder and reflect on the words of praise. She will then realize that it is not a compliment at all, that it rather points out her weaknesses, that it is a reflection of her inability and efficiency in doing the work.

When the husband and the wife realize this truth and seek to redress the situation, then their lives will be on the right track. In case this phrase lucky guy or lucky girl is used in the presence of the married couple, it could cause heartburn in one and a feeling of pride in the other.

3

The Role of Stress in Various Stages of Human Life

Stress is beginning to be a part and parcel of human existence in modern times and has become the root cause of many ailments he faces. How has it managed to manifest itself gradually at every stage in a person's life? Let us analyze the effect of stress on the following;

1. Student life and stress

2. College life and stress

3. Teenage and parents

4. Adolescence and job hunting

5. Youth and workplace

6. Salary, savings and stress

7. Looking for a life partner and stress

8. Married life and stress

9. Family life and stress

10. The role of stress in the evolution of turning one's children into school students

11. Old age and stress

The role of Stress on Students

'It is better to deweed a plant at the initial stage itself' is a universally accepted axiom. It is as students that one is susceptible to many a habit, good and bad. Like a plant that has many a weed growing along with it, so in a student's life, many different habits are likely to take root.

The child, as a student, has to cope with many situations which will leave a lasting impression on him. There is an interplay of these even as he is growing up such as bad habits, lack of awareness of the outside adult world, inability to distinguish the bad from the good, anxiety about one's looks, inferiority complex, financial insecurity, the effect of the celluloid world, need for instant gratification, impatience, rebelling against the rules, overconfidence, selfish arrogance, refusing to share, inability to prioritize, lack of exercise, inability to upskill oneself and having to adjust with other students of varied mentalities. He is thus subject to stress at various levels. Hence it becomes imperative for students to overcome these temptations and to learn the ways and means to secure for themselves a safe and successful future.

Bad Habits and Customs

The changes in a child's attitude and habits begin to manifest itself from his student days. There is a huge difference between habits and customs. Habit is individual. When a certain kind of behavior forms a pattern after having taken root in an individual over time and is seen in his actions, we call it 'habit'. Customs, on the other hand, is what is enforced by society on individuals.

The customs of a society cannot change in a short period. Certain habits of the people that are accepted by the society and carried over from generation to generation with gradual alterations befitting the times they live in, and these become the customs of that society.

Customs differ from place to place, from country to country, and one race to another. There are bad as well as good customs. When the custom of one country is forced into another country with a completely different environment, it can become a bad custom there.

Be it good or bad habits, each has stress embedded in them. But then how can good habits lead to stress, one may well ask? Considering some of the good habits as ideal, we strive to imbibe them in our lives. We try to make these good habits exemplary, and what is the result? Let us look at a few examples.

We have adopted certain habits as desirable and use them in our daily lives e.g. while speaking on the phone, in the way we dress, while sitting at the table for dinner, and while hosting our guests. Towards this, there is a tendency to copy styles from other countries and wear loose dresses, transparent ones, short and mini dresses, and unsuitable dresses. This could lead to a situation where such dresses, which may be considered in good taste in one country, may be viewed from a completely different perspective in another.

At gatherings or in public places, a person wearing a dress not suitable for the occasion or the place could lead to that person being isolated or being made the center of attraction. This could lead to stress or a feeling of elation at being appreciated but it is difficult to predict whether it is going to be brickbats or adulation.

The children may be stressed or they may enjoy the festivity but the parents are under more stress than the children when the family as a whole decides to attend a function. The parents are forced to use private means of transport to attend the function as they feel that the children's dresses are not suitable for traveling by public transport. In certain cases, the family has to return earlier than intended because of the discomfort caused by the tight dresses. We tend to ignore the after effects of wearing dresses that are not appropriate for the climate of the place we live in or the place we visit.

The phase of student life is the one where they are likely to rebel against rules and established norms. The insistence on dress code for students is one result of such rebellion by the students. This period in a student's life where he claims freedom to wear whatever he wants, as he lives in a free country, is precisely the reason for all the restrictions he is subjected to. Children are brought up on the norms and customs the parents have been subjected to by society. It is as students that they begin to feel the need to be different from their parents, and their ideas. This urge to be different from the parents and to break free of their ideas, their rules, the customs and practices they follow take root and become entrenched when they enter schools and colleges.

The food habits inculcated in us as we were growing up are well known to us. With time, one tends to forget how to get over this to become adept at eating independently. Take for example the occasion when one goes to a restaurant to have food in the company of friends or family. The scenario is completely different from the one at home. One is likely to be intimidated by the dim lights, the cold, the silence all around, the pristine white table cloth, the cutlery placed strategically, some of the strange condiments on the table, and where one is not aware of who is next to you. In the midst of all this, you place your order without being fully aware of what exactly you are ordering. There are times when one waits patiently wondering in this strange atmosphere whom to ask and how to ask.

In the midst of all this, one more hurdle in the restaurant as a student, before eating and that is whether it will look good

Perspectives of Imperfection

on camera without actually considering whether it is hygienic. Taking a photo of the food and its presentation seems to give him more pleasure than actually consuming it. After the formal lunch or dinner, where you are on your best behavior, the question one usually asks oneself is whether one is satiated and whether the food was worth the amount you spent on it. But then you convince yourself that this is how it is. Some are unable to do justice to the food bought because of false etiquette. This is the truth. You spend a lot on eating out. But you are not satisfied. When this happens once too often it leads to needless stress and strain.

The belief that a family is considered complete only with the birth of children and that guests are to be treated as Gods have traditionally held beliefs in our society that have come down to us through centuries. But with the passage of time and change in customs and practices, both these traditionally held beliefs are now considered a burden. There was a time when the guests were treated as part of the family and would participate in preparing the food, eat together, and converse together as a family.

Consider today's scenario. Guests come after fixing an appointment. To welcome them for that one hour, the house is cleaned, decorated, and made presentable. A lot of time is spent on this and a lot more on making oneself presentable. With all this happening, the host is exhausted and weary. After consultation with the family, a decision is taken to have the gathering at a hotel. It is very important to realize the part children play in such a situation. They should support the parents by helping them in getting the house and the food ready for the guests. They should engage with the guests in a mutual exchange of views and ideas, instead of sitting alone in one's room. They will benefit from this in the long run, though they may think it an imposition at that time.

The Practice of Dressing Up

We observe students paying a lot of attention to their attire and also in dressing themselves up. We are born with a certain body type and structure, depending on our genes. Attempts are made to rectify these perceived defects through beauty treatments and also through plastic surgery.

Once the children leave the house to attend school and observe other children, there is a heightened urge to pay more attention to one's appearance. This is but natural. They would want to be well-dressed like other children. This is not wrong. To wish to emulate a well-dressed person with a sculpted body and dignified bearing is a desire most kids have. Towards this, some would wish to change their very body structure. Though this is not wrong in itself, it could lead to mental stress and strain which need to be addressed by taking care of one's health and well-being.

Some decide to undergo surgery to look better. Some women refrain from even drinking water at a function as this might spoil the lipstick and the makeup. Ignoring or restricting the intake of water could lead to serious health issues. Not using the restroom because of the dress you have worn could also lead to health issues. The important lesson here is not to give up on your bodily comforts for the sake of appearances. This is the surest way to avoid mental stress.

You should take up regular physical exercises if you want to look good. You will realize how good you look if your blood circulation is on track with regular exercise. Looking into the mirror first thing in the morning after getting up from bed and feeling that you don't look good is a mistake all of us make. It is imperative for everyone to know this medical fact that one does not look one's best first thing in the morning as the blood circulation has not yet resumed its normal regular flow. This habit is best avoided. Having a nutritious and balanced diet at regular intervals is a better option than using cosmetics to enhance your appearance. This would prove to be a more sustainable solution. Taking recourse to suggestions on the internet or blindly following advertisements to look attractive is not advisable as this could lead to serious consequences.

Resorting to artificial means to streamline one's external appearance is not the right course for better looks. The color of the skin, the wrinkles on your neck, the silks you wear, or other dresses are not the pointers to your beauty. When your brain, your heart, and your liver function normally, you will look your best. Hence, it is much more important to follow a nutritious and balanced diet and regular physical exercises to maintain good health than to take recourse to enhance or improve one's outward appearance. Your good health will be reflected in the glow on your face. People, these days, attach more importance to the short-lived success of their efforts for instant outward gratification than to good health and forget about the long-term benefits of a good diet and healthy lifestyle. The inevitable consequences of this on their health, leading to various ailments and thereby on their looks impacts negatively their mental health and lead to stress and strain.

One has to adopt all possible measures to be happy in this life. You have to rise above those times when grief strikes you, by adopting and accepting universal truths. Come to terms with grief by realizing that such things happen, they cannot be avoided. Patience and the belief that time is the best healer will help one tide over the difficult times. No one on earth is free of worries. Only those who can see the positives, even in a trying situation, can succeed in life.

You cannot equate one's external appearance with discipline. Working on your looks and working on one's discipline are vastly different. Discipline as a way of life is very important for a student and life beyond his student days. Everything in life, such as your education, and your values, is lost if you have no discipline.

This important life lesson is incorporated in one of the verses in the famous Thirukkural which when translated reads, ' Discipline leads to propriety in conduct and so guard it with your life'. Sometimes even the highly educated are likely to lose their prestigious jobs because of lack of propriety or discipline in their conduct.

This life of ours is a very simple one. It is not governed by external factors alone. You must learn which vitamin is needed for bright and sharp eyes, what is needed for long, dark, and lustrous tresses, how to keep your skin shiny, and healthy, and the measures to be taken to not lose your eyesight and having learned all these, are we able to follow the prescribed healthy diet tips or restrictions? We don't and that is where we fail. Because if we do, we are sure to succeed in our efforts and that is the ultimate truth.

Propriety or Discipline while Using the Telephone

Telephones and mobiles help us stay connected to the outside world in our daily lives. The mobile has become such an integral part of our lives that we feel incomplete without it. We feel lost and helpless without it. The mobile gets updated almost every hour, what with technological advances that seem to happen in leaps and bounds. The mobile users want the latest in mobiles. This is not wrong. But while we want the latest, do we make any effort to update ourselves with the technological advances? We try. We must observe one thing and that is, we handle the latest mobile of a certain brand irrespective of one's age. Each one's handling of the mobile is different depending on their habits and practices. Hence, when there is a disagreement here, these differences should be made known very delicately and diplomatically. No one is an expert in the use of the latest mobile technology. So when there is some incident in the use of the mobile, it is better to ignore it and not make it a huge issue. Otherwise, this could lead to one losing one's happy-go-lucky nature and result in mental stress. To be able to lead a stress-free life, one has to be open about things and have a positive attitude in life.

Parent's Opinion about Schools

The first thing that comes to one's mind when we talk about student life is the school. Parents go through a lot of preparation before sending their children to school. They prepare themselves for the idea of the child attending school, the finances needed, safety and other aspects, and the standard of the school, before the child starts school. The parents take this very seriously as the child steps into the outside world for the first time away from the parents. They even prepare a classroom atmosphere at home to give the child a head start in schooling and also take precautions regarding the child's health.

Questions and thoughts like does the school have the necessary recognition; what is it ranking among other schools; what is the educational standard of the school; what employment opportunities does the school offer; how disciplined are the children; what are the safety standards; do they have qualified teachers, were never considered by parents while seeking admission for their wards. Such questions did not arise then because parents had implicit trust in the educational institutions. What mattered was that the admission was done, and they completed their education. It was only forty or fifty years down the line that parents realized the worth of the schools when someone in the course of a conversation said how they were lucky to have studied in that school or were lucky enough to have been taught by a certain teacher.

Stress in Educational Institutions

The ground reality these days is such that even before the students start their school they are faced with expectations from parents and the school. It is a fact that the expectations from the school are paramount for the parents.

The children face severe stress and pressure as students because of the expectations of 100% outcome from parents and school authorities in every aspect of school life, whether in academics, success, job opportunities, support from the management, and cleanliness and hygiene. Given that these expectations from the school are mandatory, the children are anxious and worried about his family's status, the fees to be paid, his dress and appearance, and whether these will affect his standing with his classmates.

Meaningful education happens when the goal of the educational institution is to inculcate values to lead a life, in the children and not just score high grades. Scoring a high grade depends on many factors and not everyone can expect to get such grades. This is not hidden from anyone. But it is also true that these high expectations gradually begin to play havoc on a child's psyche. Comparisons with his classmates and their performance only increase this stress and it is no surprise that when he finally passes out of the school, he is a much embittered soul. The reason for this is the expectation of 100 % success in everything. Two important questions should arise in your mind as you finish your schooling - will this 100% score help me in real life or will my intelligence when I face the realities of life? Serious thought should be given to these questions if the student wants to lead a meaningful life.

A Parent's Evaluation of the Child's Future

Parents start planning for their children's future even before they complete their school education. They expect their children to become scientists, engineers, doctors, or leaders. Towards fulfilling this, the parents ensure that the children get the requisite training by sending them to coaching classes. But what happens here? The children do not get enough leisure time to relax. The work pressure is such that they are subjected to huge mental stress. It does not end there. When they fail to clear the entrance exam or do not make it to the expected grade, the pressure mounts, resulting in the children taking recourse to extreme measures, as is evident from the daily news reports.

What is needed here? Each child is different. His skill sets are different. Forcing the child or being stern with him to make him do what the parents want will not help. When they are forced against their will to do what the parents want, they may complete the course but carry such a dislike for what he was forced to do that they may try to change the course of their life to a different path. He will have no use for the course he had studied. He may even blame the parents and lose his peace of mind. He may not get the job he aspires for. There are many instances where even after his marriage, he becomes dependent on his parents to help him lead a decent life with his family and for their daily needs. What is the reason for all this? The reason is the importance and expectation given to achieving 100% results.

We think that the teacher who teaches extremely well, gives notes, and forces the student to study is perfect in his work. But is he? Does his perfection in his teaching have the desired effect on his students? Not at all. There is a negative impact on the students. It is true that the student who works hard and spends all his time preparing for the exam may be a topper and win laurels for his achievement. However, a student who has not been taught to think independently will find it difficult to face the real world without the teacher's guidance. This is not the right way of educating a child.

Without the ability to think independently, the student, when he steps out into the real world, is bound to falter. Hence it becomes imperative for the teacher to impart his lessons keeping in mind the child's skills, his strengths, and by providing space for him to develop his intellect. Through this, he learns to think independently and is prepared to meet the challenges of life. At the same time, the teacher should be careful not to burden the child beyond his capacity which would lead to stress and strain.

4

Adolescence and Stress

Mental stress begins to take root in various ways from the beginning of the adolescent stage in a child's life. It is also in this stage that the children learn to deal with the pressures and pulls of life. The child, as long as he is a school student, is under the strict supervision and protection of his parents. When he enters the portals of a college, he faces an entirely different environment and faces many problems and challenges. It would be more appropriate to say that he realizes he has more responsibilities in this adolescent stage than problems.

He now steps out into the adult world, away from the secure family environment. He finds that there are occasions when dealing with friends, relatives, and the public at large, he begins to develop a certain bitterness, some irritation towards others. This could be because of his immaturity, his inability to make correct assessments, or making unjust comparisons. Some can rise above this by accepting that there are bound to be people who will criticize no matter what. And then some take this to heart and discuss it with parents, building up unnecessary tension. Only he who can take this in his stride and not let it affect him, but concentrate on his set goals will succeed in life, is the undeniable truth.

There is no life without problems, and problems are plenty. It is how one deals with these that determines how peaceful one's life will be. The student who makes these issues huge and refuses to find a way out of it is only trying to wriggle out of the situation without having to find a solution. Sometimes parents are not aware of the real situation here and they are at a loss to find a solution, resulting in disappointments. When the child comes with a problem, the parent has to pay heed to it by listening attentively, realizing the importance of the problem in the child's life, and trying to resolve the issue.

The mental stress becomes acute when it is examination time. What is the reason for this? It could be any of the following - a shortcoming in classroom teaching or the system in a college with not enough tests for the students or insufficient attention to studies by the students. The students tend to keep postponing the daily tasks till it becomes an insurmountable burden at exam time. He will only try to find excuses for the situation, blaming the parents, giving way to short-tempered outbursts, and finding ways and means to escape from studies, but will never accept or admit that it was all his fault.

Consider what is happening here. In spite of his temper tantrums and the numerous excuses he tries to find, the realization that there is no escape from studies and that it is his responsibility and the truth that it is he who has to face the examination makes him restless and confused. They are unable to find a solution for this situation they find themselves in. This is when mental stress enters their psyche and results in confusion, weariness, sleeplessness, anger, and disgust with themselves and one's parents. Unable to escape this mental condition, they return home after the examination. Parents deal with this either by trying to douse this tension in the child in a peaceful way or aggravating the already volatile situation by adding fuel to the fire.

Other than hoping that the tests get over as soon as possible, there is nothing much the parents can do to help the child with his studies. There is some peace and rest after the tests are done with the parents while the student spends this time catching up on his sleep. Here the parents are under further stress as they wait for the results of the examination.

Under the circumstances, how does one pull oneself out of this stress? Here parents must pay particular attention to one aspect i.e. advice. Stress arising out of studies and education is common. Parents should avoid nagging their children over this. Some children, being patient by nature, may pay heed to their parents' constant advice and internalise the same. Parents must understand that their children take after them and are more or less just like them. Keeping this in mind, the parents should introspect and ask themselves how they would react to such constant advice. Are we able to take kindly to such advice? If not, are we qualified to advise others? Having realized this, they then should stop advising and nagging their children.

Secondly, having a friend circle is a big help as friends are the best stress busters. Their gender, age, and whether they stay close by or far away is immaterial. It is advisable to approach them in person or over the phone to seek their help to relieve your stress.

Having a negative attitude to life and its challenges will prove to be a hindrance to one's progress. Your friends may not always be around to support you. Instead of being dependent on your friends or other external factors, it is better to rely on one's mental resources and develop the same to relieve stress. Nature is the best weapon to lessen stress and to develop a positive attitude to help deal with it.

Nature being the best weapon to destress, one needs to become part of nature and learn to appreciate various facets of nature. It may be plants and trees; it may be the blue sky overhead or the seashore. Nature has so much to teach us. Appreciating the beauty of the clouds floating in the vast canopy of the sky may inspire a person to become an artist, another to find comparisons with humanity while observing the trees and one may learn to live a disciplined and simple life as he watches the flora and fauna in nature. He may learn to never give up but be persistent like the waves that dash ceaselessly against the shore.

In the adolescent stage, one should learn from nature and our environment to adopt measures to lead a stress-free life. If one fails to do so, then instead of gaining victory over mental stress, mental stress will gradually gain control of your life. For instance, by the time you start looking for a job, your mental stress will have a certain goal that you cannot shake off. This mental stress will play a huge part in your married life creating tension between the partners.

Hence, if you consciously learn to overcome the mental stress in the adolescent stage itself, you will be able to deal easily and confidently with stress when you encounter it. Adolescence and college life are crucial stages in a child's life as he learns to try and deal with stress.

Adolescence is that stage of life where the child is under a lot of stress and also makes life stressful for the parents. This is the stage in his life when he learns about perfection and imperfection. He also learns that he has imperfections in him. He also learns that imperfections have their charm and that they instill the desirable quality of humility in us.

   Perspectives of Imperfection

The inclination to make comparisons is inevitable in this stage of his life. We are all different from one another with unique characteristics and have different theories about the various aspects of life. We are all humans but are vastly different from each other. Even those who have some physical deformities do not indulge in this undesirable habit of comparing with others. One with just one hand will refrain from comparing himself with those with two hands. This is because he has come to terms with this defect of his. While those of us who are blessed to have been born with no infirmities indulge in making comparisons.

Comparisons based on outward appearances, such as one's gait, dress, and attitudes are routinely made by us. We are different from one another in each of these aspects. How one is dressed, how fashionably one is dressed, how academically qualified one is, and how wealthy one is have all been made areas of comparison. What happens then?

He develops an inferiority complex. He tries to achieve his aim in the shortest possible time through shortcuts/unfair means. They use the information available on the internet. They turn to cosmetics and fast food for their gratification. Of course, they also get useful information that benefits them, but then there are those who, using the same information, harm themselves. The resultant mental stress is different because it is entirely of his own making. This mental stress may sometimes be not known to others. It manifests itself as a problem and by then the mental stress may have become more intense.

The inferiority complex that he has developed within himself that he lacks perfection now takes hold of him. He now wants perfection and he will do whatever is necessary to attain it. This is when he realizes what is perfect and what is not. This stage is when he comes out of his comfort zone and begins to understand the realities of life. He has to understand what is health and what is needed to make a person healthy. Beauty is only skin deep, and a healthy mindset is a prerequisite for beauty. He has to be in harmony with the society he lives in. Apart from the dress you wear and your healthy/ perfect body, what lends you beauty is your harmonious living with the society you live in. The wrinkles in your neck, the glasses you wear, or your expensive silk dresses are not signs of beauty. But beauty is when your brain, your heart, and your liver function well and you live a healthy life. This is the truth and once you realize this, you will be able to lead a stress-free life.

Parents and Adolescents

The world views adolescence thus:

Adolescence is that stage of life when the child is engaged in structuring his entry into the adult world in the best possible manner. This is the age when he realizes his full potential, with his enthusiasm for sports and with his energy but also has to rein in his rage/anger and curb his urge to be a hero. He wants to chart the course of his life on his terms. He is ready to take on the world and change it. A nation's wealth and strength is a measure of the power of its youth. It is the youth who bring laurels to the country with their contribution. It is an established truism that adolescence is the repository of his boundless talents.

How successful one is in bringing about these changes depends on the path one chooses in his adolescence. The way the youth looks at the world is vastly different from that of others and in the same manner, the way the world or the society looks at an adolescent youth is also different.

This is the age when society judges a child on his attitude, his manners, and his dress. The standard tools used for such judgment are based on the societal norms of that place and the region. This is the age when the youth is burdened with additional restrictions placed on him. This is the age when the youth rises above these restrictions, manages the situation, faces the challenges boldly, overcomes them, and emerges victorious. At the same time, this is also the age when along with academics the child has to chart his course in life with due diligence and to think seriously about the ways and means to achieve his desired goal. Thus he subjects himself to added mental stress himself.

The early stages of adolescence are a period in the child's life when he tends to be a lot more secretive than before. An exaggerated quality attributed to the pre-adolescent child is that the child in this stage will insist that whatever he does is right even when the societal norms term it improper. They, in this stage of their growth, are in no position to discern the right from the wrong. They gradually begin to resent their parents, their attitude, and their lack of support for their ideas. They refuse to accept the conclusions arrived at by the society. They undergo mental stress when they muster the courage to go against the established social norms, rules, and taboos.

Under these circumstances, the interaction between the parents and the child may appear strange. They expect perfection from each other. The pre-adolescent child pays serious attention to his parents' actions, their evaluations, the pattern of their acceptance, their expectations, the ability to make decisions as also their competence in time management, wealth management, the understanding between the husband and wife, and their weaknesses.

The youth pays a lot of attention to the parents' opinions about him, their confidence in him, and their expectations of him. This is the age when they will look for ways to find fault with their parents despite the parents' best efforts. Why do they do this? What do they gain from this? Of Course, there is an answer to this.

Those who dare to find fault with the parents are those who will use it to their advantage when they want to reveal what they have done or the mistake they have made, by creating certain situations. They try to express this either through discussions or by maintaining an offended silence. They will try to show their parents in a very poor light. When this happens, the parents ignore the child. This brings on added mental stress on the child as he finds himself unable to give expression to his problem. A solution to this kind of situation is easily found, if the parents and children understand each other. There are also times when the whole family finds itself under severe duress when the child takes it to extremes.

Attempts should be made to find a way out of this situation. Parents should approach the issue with a clear vision and long-term perspectives. If one has a proper evaluation of the parent-child relationship,this issue can be mitigated, to a certain extent and peace can prevail when there is an atmosphere of love and affection in the family. It is the parents who are at the receiving end in this context, since no matter what, whether there is closeness and affection or not, the adolescent child is quite capable of creating such situations.

Another area of conflict arises when the youth, with no idea of the ground realities of the family's status, tends to compare it with other families. This leads to a lot of irritation in the parents. When the parents talk about how they have provided for the comforts, facilities, and financial needs of the family, the youth tend to play it down, saying that it is their duty to do so and that all parents do this for their families, making them feel small and insignificant. There are reasons for this. Those who have lived under the protection and supervision of their parents and having completed their education with the parents' help continue to live with them are the ones most likely to feel this.

The reason for this? Parents are ready to spend for their child's education. But are concerned about the impact of such expenses on the child, especially when there is a decline in the attitude of the child towards his education and his discipline. When the expectations that the child will reap the benefits of his education are not met, that is when the blame game starts. This happens because of expectations. Here too parents expect 100% perfection. Each one of us is different in the way we perceive things and the way we work. The areas of excellence are different for each one of us.

Unlike in earlier times when a lot of importance was accorded to a particular occupation, the times now are such that diversity is welcome. New avenues and opportunities are available, and people do well in their chosen fields depending on their capacities. For instance, these days, online services, e-service apps, e-food delivery apps, and e-sports apps are available. The youngsters engage themselves in such occupations as per their talent and eligibility.

When an educated and qualified student engages in such jobs, the question arises naturally in the family as to why he should take them up. This results in the development of an inferiority complex in him. When he is not able to meet the expectations of the family and society, he is likely to get depressed. One who is able to stand up to the criticism is sure to succeed. There are those who chart their course in life through online marketing.

All this is welcome. But then why does man look at different things from different perspectives? The reason for this? Money is not the only criterion. It is erroneous to think that money is the only means to lead a secure and safe life.

Society expects propriety and good character too from men. To think that you can lead a comfortable life if you have money is a fallacy. Are you qualified for this job? Only a person with these qualifications is eligible for this job. Given these parameters, getting a job is not easy as there are certain criteria and qualifications mandated for each job.

Mental strain and stress do not differentiate between the multi-millionaire and the daily wage laborer. In fact, it is the super-rich who are more subjected to depression. How should an adolescent, face this challenge? Towards this, he should learn to cultivate an awareness about himself, his family, friends, relatives, and his community as he steps into this stage of his life, even as he completes his college life. This is even more relevant to those who have no knowledge of the outside world, having completed their education from the safety and confines of their homes.

Some of the things these children should keep in mind are:

They should give serious thought to and learn how they were brought up and who were the ones who brought them up from birth to this stage of adolescence. Consider how you have reached where you are now from where you were earlier. Think of all those who, having met all your needs as you were growing up, are responsible for introducing you to your community as a well-dressed, well-nourished, well-disciplined individual.

Having given careful consideration to all these suggestions, you should not ask yourself this question. If I were given all these facilities, which I enjoyed thanks to my parents, would I be able to do as good a job as my parents did in bringing me up? This is a sixty-four-dollar question for which there is no easy answer. Instead, you will find yourself even more confused but you are sure to find yourself at peace with yourself. Such reflections on the past will help you see the future more clearly. Questioning yourself from time to time is a good way to make your life better as you go forward. You will find that you have matured as you focus on improving your life and not waste your time on irrelevant questions.

The youth now becomes more responsible. As he begins to shoulder these responsibilities he finds that he has hardly any time for idle talk or its attendant problems. He has to face each issue carefully and think about it seriously. This will surely lead him onto the path of success in his life. In this stage of his life, if he fails to recognize his responsibilities and does not initiate the necessary changes in his attitude, he will find that he may have to wait for a very long time to settle down to the steady phase of life.

Some of them, thinking along these lines, may resort to shortcuts to make easy money, focusing all their attention and abilities on this pursuit. This happens because he compares himself to a few others in his society who have made it big, and he wants to attain that status for himself too, come what may. This is not the right thing to do. You must set a goal for yourself. You must have a proper mechanism, and a method to attain this goal. You will find immense pleasure in your success if you follow honest means to achieve this.

For instance, you grow a tomato plant, water it daily, and nourish it with manure and other nutrients. The yield you get maybe just a few tomatoes, maybe a kilo or half a kilo. There will be those who question whether the result has been worth the effort and energy you put in, in growing it. But the impact this has on your psyche is immeasurable as you feel a renewed energy and enthusiasm in your efforts. The process of growing a plant, nurturing it, and watching it flower and bear fruits is a pleasure in itself. The physical labor involved in this and the resultant fatigue is instrumental in ensuring a healthy mind and body for you. When he thus finds himself in harmony with his mind, it almost eliminates any chance of him being subject to mental stress and strain. In totality what he gains is not the profit from the sale of tomatoes. What he gains, directly or indirectly is immeasurable, it is not quantifiable. This is what is called impact or outcome. Seeking an outlet for his emotional and mental stress, a person earning in crores, will splurge his money in such activities for temporary relief. There is nothing wrong with working for an hour or so and expecting a suitable reward for his work. But here what he gets as a reward is good health which is an invaluable asset.

Hunting for a Job

Once the child has finished his graduation, he starts looking for a job, and his dream is to find a job that is commensurate with his qualifications, a job that will fetch him a good salary, a dream that is driven by an inner urge. This is when he begins his life as an individual in his own right when he starts charting the course of his life on his own.

How does stress make its entry into his mind here? It is true that he enters the race, the competitive challenge, the moment he starts looking for a job. He has to prove his worth and succeed as he competes with others for the job. This is the first step in the build-up of stress within him. The personal interview is a challenge everyone has to face while hunting for a job, whatever his academic standing may be. The interview-induced stress may be an immediate one but it is temporary. After the interview one is likely to return to one's normal state after having undergone a lot of stress before and during the interview. Why then does one have this mental stress? There are reasons for this.

It is the time frame imposed by the society on its members. This places immense mental pressure on a person who has completed his studies and has settled down in life with a steady job. Society has laid down a timetable for its members that once you cross this stage, you are expected to get married and start a family so as to keep up with other families or with the society you live in.

Secondly, a man-made unnecessary, and imaginative scenario is the belief that before considering marriage. One must have attained a certain position in life, must be drawing a good salary, and must have a healthy bank balance, and all these are necessary to lead a comfortable married life. The truth is that man's desires are insatiable, even if he is happy with his job.

It does not follow that if you have money you will be comfortable. There is no correlation between the two. There are those who lead a comfortable life with no money and then there are those who are not able to lead a comfortable life even though they are very wealthy. It all depends on one's mindset. If then this is the case, why isn't everyone able to reach this level of comfort? How can this be achieved?

Another way to get around this situation is to have a study group with friends who share your views. You can discuss and analyze the lessons with them for a better grasp of the concepts. This way you not only get to understand the lesson easily but also finish learning on time and at a lesser cost. But it also depends on your friends' circle. It is just as easy to raise your standard as for your grades to fall. Hence you have to pick such friends whose support and company will benefit you academically when you are confident that combined study with them will help you achieve higher grades. It is only those ready to accommodate the points of view of others who can do well in combined study circles.

Be positive. Learn to do away with negative thoughts. Supposing you, on your own, have studied and now are appearing for the personal interview. There will be ten people on the interview panel who are proficient in specific subjects unlike you who have studied all the subjects at the college level. When you attend an interview, you can take comfort from the thought that they will not ask questions beyond your qualifications.

You can ace your personal interview if you do not make the interviewees uncomfortable by asking irrelevant questions or questions that are in contrast to the ones they may ask. This way you are giving them negative impressions about yourself and when you do that you are sure to get negative results. But if you follow these steps you are sure to do well in your personal interviews.

Even after the interview do not review the negative points. What needs to be done at the end of each interview is to update your knowledge. In the interview, you may have faced questions for which you did not know the answers and that does not matter. But what is important is that you be prepared with the answers for the next interview. This is the cue for progress.

Self-discipline is very important. You are expected to project a certain personality when you appear for a personal interview. There is a dress code that the candidate is expected to adhere to, for each interview. The way you walk, talk and your attitude should reflect your personality. You could fail in the personal interview if your dress is not appropriate for the occasion.

After every test, there is a sense of peace and calm in one's mind. This peace of mind could turn to confusion and conflict if the results are not as expected. One should be able to rise above this and look for ways to perform better the next time by being patient and not accepting defeat.

While on the job hunt, apart from concentrating on the interview, one should also cultivate hobbies and physical workouts. You may choose the one you prefer and focus on building and maintaining a healthy body. Only when there is harmony between mind and body, will you be able to achieve your goals and attain success in your life.

Stress at Workplace

The place where one spends the highest percentage of one's life is at the workplace. His family life depends on the environment at his workplace. He starts his working life with a lot of expectations. His primary concern as he enters this phase is that he gets a job that is commensurate with his educational qualifications.

This concern begins to change slightly as he starts working in his office. No one gets a job that is a hundred percent deserving of his educational qualification. The truth is his job demands that he adjust his work as per the requirements of his workplace. It is such adjustments in this environment that will ensure that his workplace is stress-free and that his family life too is free of disruptions.

He has to establish a working rapport with his colleagues at his workplace. Their help and support are needed to carry out one's work smoothly. He has to maintain a comfortable working relationship with them with his attitude of caring and sharing for a healthy atmosphere at the workplace. If he is not able to maintain this kind of balance with his colleagues, he is sure to subject himself to a lot of mental stress as this will increase the burden of work on him and also unnecessary pressure from his colleagues.

At any workplace, one has to abide by the rules and regulations. Some may consider this unnecessary. These rules and regulations help us to complete a specific work within a specific time. They also prove to be a helpful instrument for one to become mature in their dealings not only at the workplace but also in the outside world.

It is not possible for anyone to oversee their work every minute of the day. Hence, one has to observe the rules and regulations of the workplace as well as self-discipline. You have to work with dedication till you are satisfied that you have done a good job of it. There will be a few who may mock your sincerity, but it should be ignored. Your sincerity and self-discipline may not fetch you immediate results but it will definitely benefit you in the long run.

Your colleagues at your workplace will have different mindsets. You cannot expect them to possess qualities you consider desirable. Different mindsets and issues of various nature are a part and parcel of every workplace. It is not possible to change the mindsets of others. You cannot erect a fence to stop every breeze that blows is an old Tamil proverb which when translated means that it is not possible to provide for every contingency that may arise. Give and take is a sensible policy to lead a stress-free life. There is no gain in either opposing them or talking ill of them. On the contrary, it may have a negative impact on your health.

If you are blamed for something or subjected to a disrespectful slur, accept it without demur at first as there is no point in direct confrontation. Learn to deal with it calmly and use it only when necessary. You will prevail over the others when you deal with the issue patiently and at the right time. Patience is a quality that is paramount here. Those who are patient will one day rule the world, according to a Tamil proverb. Patience is the virtue of the wise. Let us march forward. We will find success.

Do your duty and leave the rest to God. If you do your duty with due diligence you are bound to benefit. It may not be immediate but it is imminent. This is a universal truth. There are few who are ready to forego their dignity and self-respect for power or pelf or for promotion in the workplace. Having done this once, they will keep doing it even for minor benefits. Why? What for? When you think about it, you realize that it is the expectation of a higher post and the perks attached to it that serve as a propellant.

Though the higher post may give him a sense of satisfaction, it also results in mental stress due to the pulls and pressures of the conflict, on his peace of mind. Finally, they realize that what they have lost is much more than what they have gained. You caught the fish but lost your life, is it worth it, is the question.

Promotions are needed at the workplace. But what you achieve at your workplace should benefit the society. If you're looking only for personal gains without doing what is expected of you by society, then you are failing the society you live in. For this just the promotion at the workplace is not enough, you must have certain virtues too.

Income, Savings and Stress

How to make money is the priority for each one of us born on this earth and money is the only means for a comfortable life. This is a wrong notion. Man subjects himself to mental stress and suffers from ailments as his constant need is to make money and how best to save this money that he has earned. Money is the means of exchange. Saving money as money does not serve any purpose. The money earned should be exchanged for products that will serve his needs and towards build his health portfolio. Just accumulating money will not result in leading a comfortable life. Indeed this could lead one to harm or loss, even to the extent of leading you to the nether world/ depths of depravity.

You have to think twice if someone says that wealth will take you to the heavens. The path to heaven opens only when the money reaches those who need it and those who deserve it. Even those who understand this do not choose to make amends before leaving this mortal world. Why then does man desire money which has this hold over us? The dealings with money that start at birth come to an end only at the time of death. Those who are able to bring their exchange to zero level during their lifetime, are said to have understood what life is. Only they will be able to live the rest of their lives in comfort.

Money is an integral part of life. People face mental stress if they do not have money for their daily needs. This is normal. This happens to everyone, rich or poor, without exception, depending on the situation they find themselves in. Worries, troubles, and burdens- can there be life without them? He is relieved of this stress when he is able to meet his daily needs with the money he has earned. This happens regularly in our lives. But when does the stress that affects one's health begin to be felt? When you have more money than you need for your daily life? It happens when you are unable to use the money that you have saved for a particular need.

It also happens when there is a dilemma on how and where to save the money you have earned. Man lives amidst problems as long as he has money. There are times when there is a trust deficit among friends because of money and this could result in the close relationship between friends getting broken. Simultaneously, a temporary relationship with an expert begins to take root and this becomes stronger.

We have also witnessed situations when the community totally isolates them due to their disgusting behavior. They could be completely sidelined by the whole world. That is the beauty of wealth. When this sidelining happens gradually he finds himself under a lot of mental stress. He is unable to find release from this stressful situation of complete isolation and this could lead to his health getting affected. He then becomes susceptible to various ailments. Why should we get ourselves into such situations?

What is money? What is life? and what are the outside limits for both are questions for which all of us have to find the answers. Our bodies retain good health till a certain age. That is its optimum level of good health. So it is with money. The money accumulated beyond that level is going to benefit others or the society he lives in. In this case, he can make his life better and maintain his health too. The lesson one has to learn right from one's youth is sharing, either in the form of cash, kind or words. This will, to a certain extent, protect one from mental stress.

Stress while Looking for a Companion

Searching or looking for something is an integral part of one's life, something you desire. Searching and waiting are two things that occupy most of the time in our lives. Why is this? It could happen because of insufficient details in what we're looking for or when you are looking for something you haven't been able to get from society. If what you are searching for is clearly defined and has detailed instructions then you can get others also involved in the search.

 Perspectives of Imperfection

Searching for a life partner is completely different from the ones discussed earlier. The reason is the absence of details not available publicly since this search depends on individual choices and preferences. There are certain parameters that are generally discussed among people such as education, job, family details, details regarding the family's property, the status of the family, etc. At the same time, as far as physical appearance is concerned, one expects to look more beautiful than oneself. This is human nature. This is what I refer to as 'hidden definitions'.

Over time, after a couple of attempts, such expectations are relaxed. This is due to a high-expectation search. After a few days, you will feel that all these expectations do not need to be given importance. When they find such a life partner, they become stressed and lose their patience after working for a few years without success. It is man's unbridled desire and unrealistic expectations that are the culprits here. Let me place an example for this before you.

Here was a man who approached a matrimonial bureau looking for a bride. The Bureau was a multistoried building. There was a poster put up there which read, "You will find here details of girls with the following qualifications and if you are looking for a better match, please proceed to the next floor." The man now proceeded to the next floor and there too he found a poster with an arrow that said for an even better match go to the next floor and so on. Finally, on reaching the tenth floor he was mesmerized to read this on his way out, " if you are not yet satisfied with any of the would-be bride's qualifications, let marriage remain a dream for you."

Man is subjected to such disaffection because of his inability to be easily satisfied. This happens only between the bride and the groom. But there is the involvement of the two families and their respective status in society. Family affairs could come in the way of the alliance even though there is an agreement between them. Mental stress makes its appearance here. These searches lead one to a stage where it is difficult to distinguish between the lies and the truth, but then the efforts to find out the truth could also land one in difficult situations. The first stage in the build-up of the mental stress would definitely be the lies, the secrecy, the concealment in exchange of details between the two families. It is an accepted axiom of life that a wedding must happen even if one has to tell a thousand lies. This is acceptable for a marriage to take place but what about its effect on the families after the ceremony? Just think about it - there need be no secrecy, no concealment if one knows all the details beforehand about each other and their families.

Some people feel that their whole life is lost because of the truths that were hidden by their partner. Their married life hasn't started yet nor has life yet been understood by them. Despite this, they behave as though the married life that has not yet started is already lost. When such comments are made by one or two people, it is better to remain calm and understand that this could happen to anyone. Time resolves all issues. The circle of time is bound to come around and benefit even those who may feel that life has dealt them a blow.

The married couple should ensure that their life is free of interference from others. How? One should be patient and calm and ask oneself whether this deserves any consideration at all. If the answer is no, then one should forget about it right away. Take a wise decision and find out the truth of the matter without letting any doubt enter one's mind. Always remember one thing. Having a life partner provides one a platform to understand and bring to fruition one's mission and vision in life. There is a possibility that it is this mission and vision that gets affected when the untoward happens. This is the greatest downfall that can happen in one's life. And the mental stress that results, because of this, is likely to play havoc with one's health.

Stress and the Newly Married Couple

Marriage is an event in which the wife selects someone from somewhere who has suitable qualifications and names her husband, similarly, the husband selects someone who has suitable qualifications from somewhere and arranges for her to be named his wife. Married life is that situation in life that brings together two signals from two different places, makes these two signals interfere with each other, and thus brings about the exchange of views between them every minute of every day of their lives.

This signal is not that of the husband alone or that of the wife. There is no scope for individual signals in married life. The single signal when the two signals interfere with each other, is the one that signals the beginning of family life. What kind of signal it is? It's beyond one's comprehension.

Where there is a meeting of two minds, it emerges in various forms like positive, negative, in-phase, out-of-phase, lagging, leading, etc. This could result in vibrations of various magnitudes. The type of vibration and its magnitude depends on the two signals that interfere with each other.

The first step in the signaling process is not just the reflection that is seen from time to time. It is something that has been lying embedded in one's psyche for eons. It is something that emerges and is encouraged to emerge just before the wedding after lying buried for centuries. It is the signal at the other end that determines when and what kind of signal will emerge from this end. When such signals take turns and enter the minds of the couple, then it results in a variety of effects on them. This needs deciphering. At the same time, this signal could lead one to depression, depending on their capacity to endure. It is our duty to conduct detailed research into this and understand how this interplay of signals results in mental stress in people.

The self-pride and misunderstandings between the two families of the couple are the reason for the mental stress in their married life. Though it happens primarily between the two sets of parents, it does impact the concerned parties. Casting aside these minor irritants and facing the dilemma of whether to go ahead with the marriage or not, the two families generally decide to go through with the marriage ceremony. The ego is a part of everyone's mental makeup. After marriage, this becomes an important and primary signal. The differences between the parents gradually make their appearance between the married couple and sow the seed of discord between them and eventually mental stress. Such families as are able to adopt a conciliatory approach, manage to avoid this discord and mental stress.

Problems surface when the married couple let the wishes and desires of their respective families to get certain things done, enter their domain. The husband and wife are capable of running their family. They are also capable of thinking independently and executing it efficiently. In spite of this, we see the two families steering them away in two different directions, depending on the status of the family. Since this happens in the initial stages of the marriage, the couple is unable to take a call on this on their own and hence support the parents, thus creating a distance between themselves. All of them try to maintain silence and suppress their anger. But this cannot last forever. Each one tries to find fault with the other, thus creating conflicts between themselves and in the midst of all this, the indirect signals that have been thrust on them only add fuel to the fire. This is of course a trick through which they, without directly mentioning it, find fault, talk about it. This is something that happens in everyone's life at every stage and this is something that is unavoidable.

One has to give careful consideration to many a thing when two people from two entirely different family backgrounds are united in matrimony. Sincerity, culture, cleanliness, way of life, communication, and discipline are all necessary but giving 100% importance to these and missing out on goals and aims in life is not a desirable end. A certain amount of discipline in both the partners is all that is needed. If one expects anything more than that it could lead to problems. People have returned home hungry, not satisfied with the cleanliness and hygiene in hotels visited. This is because we give a lot of importance to cleanliness. Dim lights, and a calm atmosphere - are these for eating or sleeping? There are many who would rather maintain silence and decorum and not eat properly. But is this necessary? One has to learn to prioritize.

In the same way, one forgets one's own culture and tries to usurp what is considered the superior culture. Discipline is necessary. So is cleanliness which is inherent in most of us. There is uncleanliness all around us. It is impossible to completely do away with uncleanliness. In such a scenario, what should one do? We have to think about how to maintain cleanliness to the extent possible and how to protect ourselves from the surrounding uncleanliness and act accordingly.

One also changes one's lifestyle completely after marriage and it is not easy to immediately understand or analyse the effects of this on one's life. It creates a certain distance from one's parents. Secondly, adopting a fashionable lifestyle takes a toll on one's health with the ill effects of dietary restrictions. We observe that one even neglects the telltale signs of ill health in the initial stages.

One of the verses of the Thirukural goes like this - the surface wound caused by fire heals but the wound caused by the tongue doesn't. Conversation is the one weapon that is used by one against the other in their married life, like a continuous barrage of fire, to hurt each other. This could go on their entire life. This is a very powerful weapon that causes immense mental stress. As a lone individual who has to score over the others, he may use bad words or words that his opponent doesn't like or those that are likely to irritate him. One has to learn to tolerate this. How?

Not by returning the barrage of insults. But by remaining calm and composed. Secondly, convince yourself that time is the best healer or that these things are a part and parcel of life. This will definitely ensure that the person who is trying to hurt you is the one who will suffer immense mental strain and stress. As a last resort one does turn to God and seek emotional release in the form of tears. The tearful appeal to God is never wasted is the belief one holds dear.

Ups and downs are inevitable in life. Only those who overcome them can succeed and move on in life. Conversely, if your life has no challenges it means that your life has been made easy for you by someone else. You cannot bask in someone else's hard work and glory. You have to chart your own course in the journey of life, face new challenges, and overcome them, and only then can you lead a peaceful life.

One enters married life with certain expectations and when these do not materialize, they tend to create unnecessary mental stress. We have to analyze these expectations and see how far they are under the circumstances in which we live. We evolve and attain the positions of father, mother, grandfather, and grandmother through natural progression in life. This is an obvious fact of life. There are some who go against this and claim that they are still young and are not ready to accept that they have become grandparents. We have to accept the inevitable as designed by nature. As a corollary, will they be ready to accept it when we say that they died young when in reality they are on their deathbed in their eighties? They will not. Hence it is better to see that we do not subject ourselves to such stress.

Family should be a self-contained unit with its own sound and fury and a life of its own. One should be able to attract the other members of the family to oneself. One should miss one's family when one happens to stay in a hotel and miss the home-cooked food should one happen to eat outside. Your house should be always in a ready state to welcome unexpected guests. That is the sign of a happy and healthy family and not prefer to stay away from the family and eat outside food.

Children and Stress

Family and life are two different aspects of human existence. Whether an individual or a married couple, the life they lead can be called life, but it can be said that a family is formed only when a child is born. Carrying a child in the womb for ten months and giving birth to it is incomparable to any on this earth. Why do we go through this? For ten months for a child? Is it because life is incomplete without a child? Is it because the wedded bliss is not enough? There is no definite yes or no answer to this. The truth is the birth of a child brings happiness and ecstasy into a family.

In spite of the excitement of marriage and family life, there is really no escape from mental stress. The reasons for this are varied. Based on modern technological advances, we try to control the child's growth, completely ignoring the benefits and results of nature on the child's growth. As it is, since marriage and its related happenings are new to him, he faces a lot of anxiety, which is only natural. In the midst of all this, he piles on more pressure and stress on themselves trying to find out if the child is growing as per their expectations. Though the well-wishers advise him not to be worried about this, he cannot shake off his anxiety. Begetting a child is not anything new. This is something that has been happening naturally since man appeared on the earth. We invite unnecessary stress by resorting to technological advances even in this issue of giving birth to children. When one is pregnant, we look for cent percent perfection, ignoring the advice of relatives and society, ignoring the customs and practices we have grown up with. We look for and practice 100% perfection in eating, in the way we dress, in the way we walk, in the way we talk, and in the music we listen to, thus bringing about a complete change in ourselves. Then there is the fear of the consequences if we do not follow these. So when we look for perfection in every aspect of our lives, it results in mental stress.

There are two scenarios - one where one begets a number of children without worrying about the future, and then one where a child is born to parents who look for perfection in every aspect of their pregnancy. This need for perfection has a cascading effect even after the child is born. This phobia for perfection is passed on to the offspring and the mental stress increases.

Why do we let this overwhelm us? The best way is to take good care of your health and then give birth to the baby. If one looks closely it will be obvious that modern technology is used for bettering the comfort levels of human life, without even considering the impact this will have on us in the future. We pile on stress on ourselves as we need to earn more and more money to improve or maintain our lifestyle. On the other hand, if you learn to take this in your stride, it will definitely lessen the mental stress and strain on your health and your resources.

The child would be most comfortable with its parents, basking in their affection and closeness. It is the child who completes the family and it is through the child that the parents will find balance in their lives. This is an important lesson for us all. As the child grows it is seen that he exhibits the same qualities as the parents and is in fact a mirror reflection of the parents. On keen observation, it will be seen that the child manages to teach the parents to be calm and collected in spite of the irritants. You cannot decry this as false. This is our child. He has to be accepted as he is. This is the best approach under the circumstances. He who understands that the child is the father of the man will excel in life.

The other thing, as already discussed, is that the child is the best means for exchanging the wealth the parent has accumulated and when he learns to do that, with equanimity of mind, he will definitely feel at ease. Once the child is born his upbringing should be the vision and mission of your life, till he becomes a responsible adult. The parents should realize that this is not a burden but a responsibility.

Children and Public Exam

We observe that the mental stress is more on the child as a student when he is in school or college. But it is also true that the parents are subjected to a lot of pressure from outside forces when the child has to appear for public exams. We have seen parents burdening their children with more work when they are already under stress with schoolwork. They force them, become sleepless, and find fault with everything. Thus, in totality, we find parents affected by mental and physical stress during these times. They pile on more pressure on the child with their advice on what to study and how long to study expecting 100% results from them.

Parents find themselves in a dilemma. On the one hand, they are worried that the child will forget all that he has learned over two years, in two hours, and at the same time, they also realize that they should handle things with more patience. Why take on so much burden? How does one avoid this? These are questions that the parents who have undergone this situation once should be better prepared with.

A child who has no set timetable for studying is one reason for anxiety. When he has no fixed time for study he is likely to postpone his study time, spending his time reading his favorite books or wasting this precious time with his friends in pleasure-seeking activities. And when it is time for the exams they find themselves under immense stress. No one can wash their hands off the situation at such a time. Furthermore, the parents are also to be blamed for not being prepared for such eventualities.

Both parents and the child should prepare themselves to deal with such stressful situations by foreplanning and forethought. Patient handling of the situation is what is needed, without both the parents and children succumbing to severe stress. The question we should be asking ourselves is why is the same importance not given to improving one's health as much as the importance we give to improving one's education? In fact, equal importance should be given to health improvement, if not more.

Having to study is a load for students. Vitamin deficiency leads to one's weak health and to remedy this situation both parents and children should pay more attention to consuming nutritious food. Group study is the other solution to destress the students about exams and education. This way you not only bring about improvement in your academics you also put an end to unnecessary squabbles or misunderstandings among friends.

Some parents who are in constant touch with their friends have the habit of comparing their children with others. No child likes to be compared or faulted. This comparison of your child with others and judging him by their standards, your constant advice should be avoided and completely stopped. Give due consideration to how your child is performing under the circumstances you provide him with.

Parents have this tendency to tell the children how they grew up, their school and college days, and that they did not have any of the facilities the children have nowadays. But what they forget is that in their days they did not have such cutthroat competition which children face these days and also the mental stress they undergo as a result. They lead a stress-free life whether at home, in school, college, or at the workplace and their children do not have even 10% of such a stress-free environment. They are not able to energize immersing themselves in nature as everything around us reeks of artificiality including our diet. Under the circumstances what you feel for the children is pity and not anger or irritation.

Self-discipline is what is needed, self-discipline in the way you dress, the way you talk, and in your attitude. Children can rid themselves of the tension during exams if they adopt self-discipline as a rule in their lives. We have seen that no results are achieved just by advice or talking about it. This is not the right way to go about it. What is the role of parents in ensuring that the children learn self-discipline? Not just by advice but by being a role model themselves can parents instill a sense of self-discipline in the children.

The external facilities provided by the parents for the children's studies may be basic. But that cannot be the reason for not being serious about his studies. Haven't children, without basic facilities, made a name for themselves, becoming leaders and high officials? The hallmark of a sincere student is when he tells himself with utter conviction that come what may, I will not fail in my duty and will challenge myself to attain success. Individuals who have such convictions can prove that they can survive in any situation. Only he who is focused and has a never-say-die attitude will succeed in his chosen path and progress in his life.

Parents should not impose their expectations on their children. They should, keeping this in mind, encourage their children to do well in their studies. Sometimes, some families use their wealth or unfair and easy ways to attain what they want. This is likely to distract the children's attention away from their studies and destroy their sincere efforts.

Parents are likely to feel stressed when their children are entering the job market because of their expectations. They should also be careful what they say about their children since the children these days don't like parents discussing them.

The child may get excellent results when excessive restrictions are placed on him during study time. But the situation he faces, when he steps out into the marketplace, trying to get things done on his own, would be vastly different. Everything he looks at is new to him. Wanting to experience them, he might take a step in the wrong direction. Hence it is important for parents to educate their children about the outside world either through an inclusive approach or through travels outside town.

Parents should inculcate in their children a love of/ for God. The child, through his communion with God, will be able to attain the peace of mind and the tranquillity needed to excel in his studies. This is an excellent way to get rid of one's mental stress. A few minutes of meditation will certainly help a person destress himself, whichever religion he may belong to. This helps the family members develop a closer bond among themselves when they get together for group meditation. The misunderstandings grow bigger when there is no bonding between the family members. The close kinship also lends an opportunity for the family members to understand the child's mentality.

Parents should praise the child for their success every time as this will encourage the child and it will also make the child realize that he is doing the right thing. But parents should not overdo this by praising the child 100% every time but be discreet in their praise. Don't give them fulsome praise just because they expect it. False praise will make the child lose interest in doing better or planning for it. Though this is difficult it has to be done sensibly so that the child feels happy about it. Parents should whenever possible explain with examples principles of general good behavior. The children should be familiar with concepts like positivity, underestimation, and selfishness so that they will be on their guard when they come across such words.

Unnecessary despair and thereby mental stress are the results when one gives in to worries, sadness, and other painful emotions. It is possible to get over these if one learns to ignore these negative thoughts. How is this possible? Is it that easy to forget or ignore such thoughts? Certainly, this is a tough ask. But nothing is impossible if one makes the attempt. Let us look at this with an example.

Walking is an integral part of our lives right from our birth. We also do this with great sincerity as exercise for good health not only the body but your legs and feel the pain. Look at it from a different angle. You feel the pain when you exercise your legs. This is the truth. But then along with this is another natural phenomenon to which no one pays much attention. No one considers the loss of energy that results when you move your hands too along with your legs when you move. This is a natural physical component of movement and its execution. There is no extra pressure on the legs because of the natural movement of our hands as we walk. In a similar vein, we should learn to ignore the inevitable pinpricks of life.

5

Old Age and Stress

Adulthood is a period of transition through the stressors of nearly six developmental stages. For a child, the mother is the beginning and end of the world. The youngster is adamant about getting what he wants. The teenager is one who demands his wants. The adult is one, going beyond all this comfort himself, saying that what he gets is enough. Parents are those who are ready to adjust, live, and move on even with what they do not have. The elderly are those who have passed all these stages of life and say they can do without anything. Finally, the super seniors are those who say in resigned tones that they do not need anything.

The elderly would have lived through nearly 60 years of changes in the world and technological advances. They would have considered the changes at every stage of their life as a manifestation of perfection and lived it. What do they wish at the end of those sixty years? Perfection? Or Imperfection? This needs to be looked into. They expect their children also to live the way they did, looking for perfection in all aspects of life. Once they are older they look for a different definition of perfection. Forsaking their search for perfection at home, comforts, and in everything, they wish to return to their childhood days, to be petted and pampered. Most parents realize that their wish to live the life they are used to, with memories of yore, with dignity and ideas of perfection will not set them free from mental stress and strain.

The word elderly could refer to both - those old chronologically and those who are mature in their knowledge and wisdom. Age is physical and wisdom is a state of mind. The attitude and the thoughts of the elderly person who has aged physically and has matured intellectually, and is at that stage of life when he is not steady on his feet and can be compared to a youngster, and you will find him slightly different. This age which has the attributes of both the youngster and the elderly is a completely different one from all the other ages of a human being.

There is a vast difference between the interest, the disposition the elderly have towards the outside world and the respect, the dignity the society accords them. They are in their second childhood, with frail bodies like children but with great maturity of mind, experience consistent mental stress, and hence they need to be supported. This stage in life is one where the elderly try to execute their thoughts and desires in the way they want.

It is worth noting that the elderly in this stage of their lives are neither able to attain their needs nor are they able to express their needs and hence are subject to a lot of mental stress.

The elderly now bestow their entire attention on others and on the needs of the family. At the same time, the other members of the family fail to give the elderly the importance they expect or deserve. The answer to the question ' why ' is the widely held view in the community that they are elderly, have lived their lives, and now we want to live ours freely and without interference or encumbrance. Thus, in this stage, the elderly are not able to prioritize their needs.

What kinds of needs do they have? What are their thoughts and desires? What is to be gained by fulfilling those? It is very necessary to know the answers to these questions. By highlighting the importance of these points, I wish to bring about an awareness in each and every family about how their elders have to be treated.

There is no escape from stress in old age and there are many reasons for this. Many parents would like to relive their younger days, keeping aside the changes they have experienced in their lives, from their childhood days, the luxuries they have enjoyed, and the path they have tread climbing the ladder of success. They would prefer the simple life they had lived to the modern facilities life has to offer them now. They would like to reap the benefits that they have accrued as a result of the efforts undertaken by them in their younger days to be physically fit, the busy life they had led, and their hard work.

But of course, in their old age, their frail body does not cooperate with them. The spirit may be strong but the flesh is weak, but despite this, most old people would love to be active and involved as they were earlier. When they think back on their younger days, it is only natural that they feel enthused by those memories. They experience a feeling of wholesomeness while talking to their old friends. Reliving old memories, the incidents those memories bring to your mind, have the power to re-energize your mind. It becomes imperative to relive one's past as a measure to destress oneself. It is even more of a must for those who have moved from their villages to the modern cities not to forget their past.

Secondly, there is pressure to change one's lifestyle due to the changes brought about by the advancements in civilization. Evolving with the times is necessary. However, it would be incorrect to completely give in to it and lead a life devoid of comforts and happiness. Civilization is for man and not the other way around. For the elderly living comfortably lies in wearing the dress they are comfortable in, and the kind of lifestyle they prefer. To this end, it is good to make sure the elders are under no undue mental stress. An easy balance is to be maintained between being comfortable and stress-free while adopting a modern lifestyle.

Thirdly, there are many senior citizens who feel lonely and neglected, without a proper support system either from the family or from society. What could be the reason for this? The elderly would love to spend their time talking with their children, their friends, and relatives. When they do this on a daily basis, we find them happy and feeling that they are a part of the family. This two-way conversation, either in person or over the phone makes them happy.

There are many households where the elderly in the family spend days without exchanging a single word with the other members. This needs to be changed. The family members should talk to each other, on a daily basis. Though this is a difficult proposition considering the lifestyle changes that have taken place in society, the benefits are bound to be huge. No one should forget that the elderly are a repository of the wisdom of life. They are a treasure trove of the philosophies of life that no book and no education can impart.

Next, we find a lot of severe restrictions on the food habits of the elderly, either due to their advanced age or on medical advice. This could result in them feeling a little low since everyone in their old age wishes to indulge in their favorite food. When they are not able to eat what they wish to or the natural food they like, they are disappointed. It becomes the duty of the family members to be sensitive to their needs and get them the kind of food they want in small quantities, keeping in mind their delicate physical condition. They express their needs and their desires when they talk to them. Accordingly, we should become their

     Perspectives of Imperfection

support system. They wish to seek wholesomeness or completion in their lives by wanting to do those things that they couldn't do in their younger days or couldn't experience then. Some express their inclination to do charity work and wish to serve but with authority. We should make all these possible for them, willingly and readily.

Further, we see that the elderly are happy to spend time with the first, second, and third-generation members of their family. It is a fact that children are more attached to their grandparents than their parents. This benefits the children in their growth and the elderly in minimizing their stress through their interaction with the children. They are able to forget their anxieties and stress when they share their accumulated wealth, be it money or their experiences with their grandchildren.

As against this, those who are forced to live in foster homes for the elderly, are cut off from the second and third-generation grandchildren and lead a lonely life. It leads to a lot of mental stress on them. It has become a common feature of modern life and is the root cause of mental stress and attendant illnesses.

There is no rigid rule about how to lead your life from your youth to old age. As life evolves over time, so will the rules and regulations regarding life keep changing. There might occur certain great changes in life due to natural calamities. Your aim should be how to cope with these changes without feeling disheartened. The facilities you have in your life are not permanent, and when one faces changes or challenges, the elderly should not let these changes affect their normal health. It is precisely because they tend to neglect their health concerns that they face a lot of health issues. They subject themselves to a lot of mental pressure when they are not able to maintain their health. How can this be dealt with? The elderly have to have a long-term vision for this within themselves and plan accordingly even before reaching this stage of their lives. To live a carefree and healthy lifestyle even after reaching this stage, they should steer their life around to live as per their long-term plan and live a stress-free healthy life.

There is a limit to the support you can extend to your family, friends, and relatives. Of course, you should help others, but not at the cost of one's own individuality. The elderly should attain a comfort level in their lives with the help of technology. Through teleconferencing and videoconferencing they can establish a support system to avoid loneliness.

Depending on how healthy one is, the elderly should undertake journeys outside the home as it provides one a chance to speak openly and freely. It also provides one with a refreshing change of scenario. The elderly should also keep changing the route they take for their daily walks.

The primary concern that arises with lifestyle changes is one of safety. Of these, self-defense, protecting one's property, and the safety of one's kith and kin are of paramount importance. Nothing we own is permanent. We must remember that every square foot of land that we stand on has been possessed and enjoyed by thousands of animals and human beings for hundreds of centuries before us. None of these belong to us. The only thing that is ours is the comfort that we enjoy and to achieve which we struggle all our lives. Once a man realizes this, he will be free of half his anxieties. For the elderly, daily meditation as a way of life is highly appropriate. Along with this, they should also develop a charitable disposition.

Change in Financial Status

The one reason that can completely change the course of life of the elderly is their financial status. Finance would refer to both hard cash and property. A time comes in the life of the elderly when they have to think of division and distribution of the property, among their children, that they have acquired over the years, and it is a time of great mental stress for them. They come face to face with a situation where their financial position will undergo drastic changes that will bring about dramatic changes in their personal lives too. This stress is not only the result of having to distribute their wealth among the family members but also because outsiders are involved in the exchange of property.

The sense of equanimity, balance, and belonging that they have acquired through financial stability gets greatly disturbed when it comes to the division of their hard-earned wealth. They are completely confused now. Not only this but the fact that they now have to reconcile themselves to a situation where they have to make do with pension as against the handsome salary they were drawing is another factor that contributes to the mental stress. That they now have to look for financial support for their needs from their children is another reason. Other than this, the changes in the rules in savings and the consequent decrease in monthly interest also makes them further deepen their depression. Financial losses also add to their stress.

All these concerns must be taken into account by the elders before they reach the superannuation stage. Most people ignore these concerns. As an earning member, they save a large part of their earnings for the family. When they have to relocate to a new place due to family circumstances, the ensuing financial adjustments to be made also lead to mental stress. In their old age, their health issues and the medical expenses incurred also affect their financial status. The changes in the economic conditions of the state or the country impact the individual at a personal level. This is beyond one's control. How does one cope with this?

One has to manage his fiscal needs in such a way that there is no great difference between the income received before his retirement and the income after retirement. He has to look for means and methods to offset the decrease in his income after retirement and follow them. Do away with unnecessary expenses to augment the income you get after retirement. Health is the best wealth. One must pay more attention to maintaining good health through regular exercise, going for daily walks, and thereby ensuring that you keep all illnesses at bay, especially diabetes and blood pressure. Eating only organic and natural food is a good habit.

Old Age and Appreciation

Everyone in their lifetime would have achieved a great many goals and would have also created achievers before reaching their retirement age. We, who at this stage are the achievers, forget the person/s who made us what we are today. Instead of thinking of this as an error, it would be more appropriate to consider it our primary responsibility. For the elderly, the appreciation he gets from the person whom he turns into a high achiever is more precious than the affection and support he gets from his family and relatives. This can be done from different platforms.

They can be invited to be part of the function you have organized or the one you are part of and acknowledge and appreciate their role in your achievement in the presence of the gathering. How beneficial the tears of joy glistening in their eyes at the open appreciation for the physical and mental well-being of the recipient is best left to the medical profession to analyze and explain.

Appreciation is an essential part of life. The appreciation and laudatory references for their sincere achievements have the ability to re-energize the elderly, and at the same time, it can have a negative impact if it is felt that they do not deserve this appreciation. This of course is temporary while the sincere appreciation will linger on for a much longer time.

There should be clarity about where, when, and how to express one's appreciation. The appreciation for the elderly can be expressed at various events or even festivals. The appreciation can be about their skill at doing things, their sense of discipline, their charitable disposition, their inclination to serve society, or to appreciate the title they have been conferred with as 'People's Friend'. There are many ways to express one's appreciation.

You ought to be aware of the individual who values you. There may be many among your customers who are worthy of praise. An appropriate occasion may not have presented itself to appreciate them. Such people should also be honored with praise. The ideal method to show your gratitude would be to do this. When expressing gratitude for someone, it's crucial to remember the moment, the place, and the person.

This brings recognition to the person who is appreciating as well as the person who is being appreciated. It is true that when we receive accolades and affection from society we also get recognised as important.

This can also be done by bringing out books in their honor or by way of articles in the media. The elderly would take heart when they think about this, and it will act as an inspiration for them on a daily basis. This also can be used as an occasion to include those left out inadvertently.That this generates immense energy and self-confidence in the elderly, if the appreciation is genuine, is true. Appreciation is of two kinds - when the youngsters appreciate the elderly and the elderly appreciate the youngsters. In the first instance, the elders feel proud, and in the second, the youngsters are encouraged and energized to build a life that will be an example for others.

Appreciation has the effect of making even frail old people stand proudly erect. After a certain age, the only permanent thing for the elderly in life is praise and that is exactly what they need. There are many results of such appreciation. It helps to bring out the broad-mindedness of the person when he attempts to praise someone for the first time. This way he will be encouraged to help and support others so that he too can become eligible for such appreciation. With their sincere wish to help others, they end up being happier. Their generosity and desire to share makes them become even more supportive. Such appreciation makes them realize that all their actions have a positive impact and are beneficial. Just think about the positivity this brings about in the lives of the elderly who long for such appreciation and praise. And all those who receive such praise should ensure that they remain worthy of the appreciation they have received.

The praise showered on someone should not be exaggerated as this might make them feel that they are perfect and may not seek to improve themselves further. It would be far better for the elderly to be realistic when they praise the youngsters and show them how to improve and grow in their chosen fields instead of using words like 'excellent' and '100% perfect'.

The family of the elderly person may know very little about his achievements or his skills. They may not even be aware of the high regard and respect he has earned in the outside world. In such a situation they will realise his worth only when his contribution and his achievements are appreciated and celebrated. So such occasions must be created for them, be it the wedding anniversary, a birthday celebration, or a wedding day. When they are honored thus, it acts as a blessing for the family and it will improve their health too.

The Benefits of Appreciation

It makes known to his kith and kin the respect and regard the outside world has for him.

It encourages others to do good for society.

It brings about a change in his overall health condition and increases his life expectancy.

His self-confidence is enhanced.

It is an opportunity to identify the deserving candidates.

It helps to forget the pricks and pains of life and to look forward to continuing to evolve and do good.

It serves to relive the memorable moments of one's earlier days.

It acts as a bridge between the outside world and the retired person confined to his home.

6

Causes of Stress

Stress and its impact on a person depend on the issues that he internalizes from his environment. No one can lead a problem-free life. The essence of a person's success and skill lies in how he deals with the problems and challenges in his life. Not melting down or breaking down in the face of challenges. The extent of his mastery over his life depends on the extent to which he faces the problems and successfully overcomes them. He is likely to face problems of twelve different kinds and at various stages. Enmity, introspection, doubting or false prediction, false accusation, attacking, oppression, isolating, withdrawing support, denigrating / insulting, overburdening, or lessening the burden are some of the problems. To come out of these, one has to practice and adapt the tools such as accept, react, divert, forgive, patience, confidence, analyze, prey, share, and vacate.

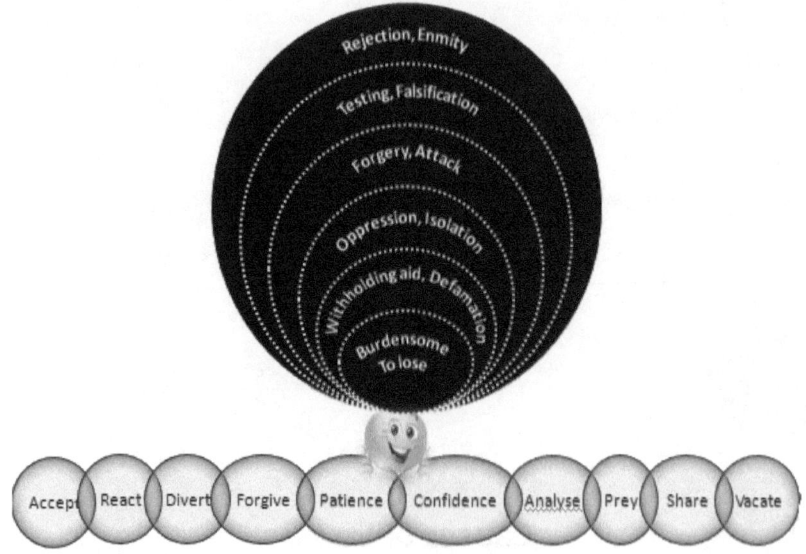

Rejection

When you have executed an idea of yours, which according to your intellect, you are well thought out, well-considered, and about which you have complete confidence, gets rejected outright by another as being imperfect and unacceptable, such rejection leads to a very unsatisfactory, unpleasant situation. Rejection can be termed as the first step of an imminent problem, a problem that is going to unfold.

Mental stress results when someone gives a wrong estimate about you, which is unacceptable to you. The backlash that you have to face in some situations if your life could be very stressful. Using one's common sense, looking for perfection, and raising unnecessary questions for which there are no easy answers is a sure-shot way of creating tension and stress within oneself.

Using various means to oppress those around you and to gain an upper hand over them, leads to mental stress on both sides. It is quite common for one to unnecessarily thrust his intellectual superiority into certain issues, leading to mental stress. Mental stress also results when one deliberately creates controversy by doing the opposite of what the other person is saying or doing. A man who has worked sincerely, without resorting to illegal means and leading a happy life may face rejection when he tries to highlight the facts of his life to the society at large, in an attempt to improve his own life further. There may be no real reason for this. But when he faces rejection every time, he is bound to be mentally stressed out. The opportunities they get may be taken away from them, and some of the facilities may also be denied to them. Attempts will be made to stall the good news from reaching them. All this happens due to jealousy and wicked intentions of some people.

Enmity

Enmity develops between two people because of misunderstandings. Apart from this, when society respects and celebrates a man, he becomes a cause for enmity for no apparent reason by a few. It is human nature. It is also because of a few qualities in us. A person who in his pursuit of perfection, develops and displays certain exemplary qualities becomes an object of enmity of those who cannot digest his standing in society. This enmity weakens the friendship in the group. And we get isolated.

It is difficult to find a reason or an answer for their enmity. When a few within the group move away, the others too, will distance themselves. The reason is the fear of them too being isolated. This enmity is also the reason why the group stops sharing and caring completely. When the number of people who are isolated gets larger, then it should become apparent that the cause of enmity is not the individual. Or if he is, he should correct himself to the extent possible.

One cannot claim that a particular person is the sole cause of the enmity. It could be that the enmity has been handed down through generations. It may take a while for this enmity to come out in the open. One has to develop the maturity to deal with this. Humans have a natural tendency to develop enmity with others right from childhood to old age. This happens quite naturally among students because of their tendency for backbiting i.e. they have this habit of spreading false rumors about others.'

    Perspectives of Imperfection

Hating someone is very easy. But what about the complications that arise thereon? What are the losses due to enmity? It is very difficult to rid oneself of the results of enmity. The positive side of this happens sometimes when, because of the enmity, one can use it to set one's life on the right path. One can also use this to get rid of certain unnecessary actions, as though enmity gives one an opportunity for this.

To harbor enmity for long is not good for one's physical and mental health. Some people might deny this, thinking that it does not cause any harm. But this is not the truth. Unknown to them, it could cause a lot of harm.

When enmity arises between us, one should ponder deeply about how to avoid it. Try to find out through others the reasons for the enmity.

When you do come to know the reason, find out if the enmity is because you have not forgiven the person, forgive him. If it is worth forgetting, do forget it. Or try through reasoning and suggestions, to resolve the enmity. But if the enmity is because of the progress you have made, just ignore them. It will continue.

You should not forgo your progress in an attempt to end the enmity.

People who are hated should not be seen as enemies.

If you feel that all those around you are enemies then the chances for finding a solution get narrowed. It could result in mental stress and affect your health. Let not the old enmities play with your life. Our parents and relatives have to play a major role in this.

Enmities between families could cost one timely help from them in emergencies. It results in a loss of affinity when one thinks of enmity or enemies. This will distract the man's attention away from progressing and improving one's life into useless pursuits. If the clouds develop enmity it may result in droughts.

Enmity results if you are not ready to extend the minimum help you are capable of. Like when you throw away excess stuff that you have, rather than share it, you will be inviting enmity. Competition in the business could result in enmity. Hence it is better to avoid enmity with a little give and take to lead a stress-free life.

Introspection/Testing

Man seeks to reveal his thinking ability and acting ability to the world. Sometimes, they are unable to express themselves. To understand the reason why it is not possible, the phenomenon of testing occurs in life. Such a test reveals one's shortcomings and the mistakes one has committed knowingly or unknowingly. Temptation is only for a few.

Of course, this does not happen to everyone. Only a few subject themselves to introspection. Sometimes it is attributed to God's intervention. If it is God who is testing you, then the test will always be proportionate to your capability and never beyond it. Here, we are subject to a lot of pressures and pulls. These testing times should not demoralize you. Many of us are stressed when tested. It should not make the person suffer during testing.

Perspectives of Imperfection

Sometimes, these trials and tribulations come in droves and overwhelm you. Their root causes are sometimes beyond one's comprehension, and this could have a crushing effect on one's life. It could make you feel that this is the end. One could be blamed for no reason, to the utter disgust of the neighbors. This could lead to such confusion that one is stressed out completely, though there is no evidence of it physically in one's outward appearance. This could last for months and sometimes even years. One should realize that this is only a testing time and that it cannot last forever and accept it pragmatically. You should console yourself saying that the trials God sends your way are only to test your endurance level and never beyond it. Such people will surely encounter a wonderful surprise at the end of it. It sometimes teaches you what life is all about. You will witness enormous peace and a huge change at the end of the period of tribulation. In totality, these trials are learning experiences and are a means to analyze the philosophy of life. What these continuous trials and tribulations do is expose you to a new way of life at the end of it. You need to be calm, collected, humble, and wise in dealing with the crisis. If you are going to use violence or suspect others for your pain due to the testing times, you will never find a closure for this. Practicing yoga or direct communion with God is the surest way to find liberation. Surrender yourself, surrender your pains. Victory is ours.

False/ Wrong Estimation and Suspicion

It is true that society sometimes deliberately gives a false estimate about people who have reached high posts due to their hard work, those who have become influential due to their academic excellence, and those who are celebrated for their admirable qualities. They are wrongly portrayed as people who have made a fast buck through crooked means, who have fake academic qualifications have bought celebratory positions through their ill-gotten wealth and who seek publicity through false propaganda, thus making them miserable. They implicate them in the eyes of the public by casting aspersions on them and by their wrongful and false estimations though they may be beyond reproach.

And when this happens within a family, a virtual rift appears between the husband and wife. Suspicion is a dangerous weapon. It could either completely isolate a person or provoke him to put up a spirited defense. We must consider our plight from different perspectives when we are ostracised or isolated from others. When one is suspected, he may lose many opportunities in life. There are times when rumors are spread deliberately about a person.

Guessing is resorted to when there is no close relationship between people. When there is no close relationship and when someone wants to take revenge on a person, such guessing or spreading rumors is resorted to. There is no need to fret/worry about this since the rumor monger gets exposed sooner or later, and the time will come when he will admit to society that he is, in fact, the rumor monger. Such rumor mongers will be ignored by the society. So let us not worry about such people who wish to destroy us. The thought that this is my life and I want to live it my way will drive away all fears of rumors. If one is aware, before the band, that these are the consequences of guessing and spreading rumors, then one will be able to manage and live life the way one wants to.

False Accusations

Indeed, the society sometimes casts a false presumption on those who are elevated by hard work, those who are influenced by their education, and those who are praised for their virtues. No one be it the elderly, a youngster, the rich or the poor are spared from this attack. There is amongst us a group of people who take great pleasure in besmirching the reputation of those who have made a name for themselves in society, by destroying their lives through false accusations. The person who is targeted, thus either in person or through wall posters or the media is staggered initially by this attack. Trying to mount an immediate counterattack, without thinking things through, will not serve the purpose. One has to explore all avenues of counterattack. Of course, if you are innocent, then these accusations will not affect you. But generally, such false accusationsdo affect one and cause mental strain and stress.

A crime needs punishment, and punishment is accorded to one who has committed the crime. False accusation, it can be said, is a punishment given or suffering inflicted on one, before the crime is proved. A false accusation is an attempt by an individual or a group of people who are familiar with your weaknesses, who know which accusation will cause maximum damage to your reputation, and who wish to show by their actions, their resentment towards you. This is not planned with an eye on immediate results. This is planned with the aim of hampering his rise or progress in his field. These are all temporary events and temporary setbacks.

My view is that one must use these false accusations and these setbacks as the basis, as foundation stones for upliftment and not for one's downfall. These are all things that keep happening in life. They are likely to disappear without leaving even a faint trace. In the temporary run, we should not let go of our duty in spite of the false accusations. Go ahead boldly. One must remember that while the forefinger is pointing an accusing finger at someone, the other three fingers are pointing at the self. We can call those who hurl false accusations at others as lacking in self-respect. These fault finders will continue with this even when they are in Heaven. There is no respite for people from false accusations. One should not be hasty while dealing with false accusations. This is because no one is aware of the reality or the truth behind these accusations. Besides, the false accusations reveal the real character of the accuser to society rather than the accused.

Attacking

The mental stress that results from the attack on one is a severe one. This is not a physical attack between two people who don't agree with each other. It is the result of the feeling of jealousy and a feeling of disgust with his own life that exhibits itself in a savage attack on the other. The beauty, status, power, and influence of a person fuels the feeling of inadequacy in one and leads to such attacks on the character of a person who has all these advantages. Our behavior, the approach we adopt in society, and our intelligence play a major role in such attacks on us. We always leave some, even if minor, way or means for them to mount an attack on us. We can save ourselves from such attacks by not associating with them in any manner either through our speech, deeds, our behavior, dress, or our expressions. The way we think and the way we make decisions vastly differ from person to person. We should be aware of such qualities in a person at least to some extent. It is rude to attack a thing of beauty because it disgusts you. But he can change himself, and his attitude if he is ready to adapt himself to the idea of beauty and to appreciate it.

It is meaningless to be jealous of a person older than yourself but much healthier, with a firm, trim body and walking very majestically. Instead, when we are such an individual, we must be inspired, even without even actually being aware of it, to be like them and we will succeed in our efforts. Just think. If you don't see such people in your locality, will you make the effort to emulate them? Not. It is true that being inspired by such people and urged by your inner self you find success and progress at every stage of your life. So even before the tendency to attack takes root in you, you should overcome it. Of course, success and progress are a product of one's inner urges. When that happens, you will find yourself appreciating your beauty, your efforts, and your traits. In order not to be a hindrance to anyone, it is enough if you follow these tips and there will be no hurdles to your success and progress in life.

Oppression

We have often heard of people being subject to oppression by others either because of their superior conversational skills or their strong physique. There are times when it starts with just talks and ends in violence. This is just a ruse. Oppression is used as a weapon to portray someone as inadequate and downgrade them, be it a colleague, a family member, or a relatives. Take, for example, a colleague at work. As friends who have been working together for a long time, all the colleagues at the workplace are familiar with the characteristics of one another. One who wants to downgrade a colleague at the workplace would know his weaknesses, and he exploits them using his persuasive skills. Though these are temporary incidents, and even if the argument lasts just a few minutes, its repercussions are many. We know that unnecessary confusion and the inability to express inner turmoil gradually result in severe mental stress.

Most quarrels begin based on the qualities one does not like and the topics that one hates. That the opponent can be provoked using such words would be known to them. But then those who seek to oppress others do not get the kind of response they want. On the other hand, they are certain to lead a life without relief or peace. If one continues in this vein despite being aware of its consequences, it will indirectly affect your life. Do not fall prey to oppression. Set a goal for yourself. To fight for that and to emerge victorious should be our aim. Think deeply about the remote possibility of someone finding a way to oppress you and destroy the same. Success is yours.

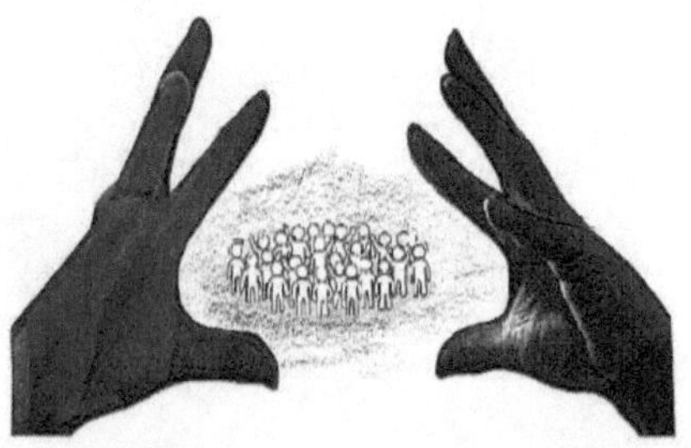

 Perspectives of Imperfection

Isolating

Loneliness plays an important role in creating mental stress in one, and the relief for this lies in sharing with others. A person who is completely cut off from others will find his loneliness unbearable. Some people may use this to take revenge on their opponents. A person who has been thus isolated, be it in an office where you work in a group or a joint family or in a classroom, will be so affected by it that he will find it difficult to adjust to the situation and all his attention will be on the effects of being isolated instead of concentrating on the job at hand. But this is not going to help. All of us need a medium, a channel of communication for sharing our joys and our anxieties. This support system may be a chosen group of friends, a set of trusted colleagues, family members, or even the elderly. We must establish such a support system.

He will not be allowed to voice his concerns. His actions and his abilities will be hidden from the outside world. As time goes by, we may even start wondering if such a person does exist amongst us and if he is indeed a part of our circle of friends or colleagues. What is the reason for this? Honesty and harmony are the qualities generally expected in a workplace. We may be honest, but we forget to work in tandem, in harmony. Working in harmony becomes very essential when a group decision needs to be taken and in its absence, when a person is unable to work harmoniously with others in the group, it will lead to a situation where he will be isolated.

In some instances, you will find yourself deliberately isolated in spite of your honesty and harmonious nature. This is something you cannot avoid, but this is not something you need to worry about. List out the opportunities to find solace/ comfort/ cheer in solitude. Be positive about it. Think of it as a God-given opportunity. Try to carry out one by one the things you have listed without any hindrance. You will find such fulfillment as you have never experienced before. You will find inner peace and tranquillity. Mental strain and stress will vanish into thin air. You must know for sure that it is your self-confidence and sustained effort that will determine your success or failure in this endeavor.

Withdrawing Support

A person who is isolated may even find his privileges snatched from him. Withdrawal of support often happens when you are doing exemplary work for the society or for the country with the help of people in high offices/ in positions of authority. This is in a way, a ruse to create tension. This is done as a first step to destroy the reputation and fame of one by another using one's influence. They would approach the concerned authority and by spreading wrong information and false accusations, withdraw the promised support. This is an everyday affair, even if you are sincere. We have to be careful. The promised support could be withdrawn anytime. It is best to be prepared and adjust accordingly as otherwise it will lead to disappointment and mental stress at the wasted effort. It is possible to get the work done in two or three stages if one is aware of the possibility of withdrawal of support. Be ready with an alternative/option.

This way the work can be done without hindrance and this will be a lesson for those who wish to trouble us.

Denigrating/Insulting

Denigrating is a weapon used to destroy the reputation of a person who has earned a good name in society. Besides, it is also used to project oneself, one's wealth, one's skills, influence, and one's popularity by denigrating, in the presence of others, the person whom he wishes to destroy. Such a person would have internalized the undesirable qualities of backbiting and telling lies. They indulge in self-praise. They are like the fence that ate the crops kind of people. Though they may praise the beauty or appreciate the status of a person, they are more interested in bringing down others' reputations. Though they are wise, they gradually lose their respect and standing in society because of this tendency to denigrate others. How we react and respond to the denigration is important.

When two people meet, they may not exchange insults. One may be from a rich family and the other from a middle-class family. But the thought keeps going through their minds as to how they are introduced and how well they are treated. If anything is said or done that is not in keeping with his status, it is taken as an insult. What was said or done may not have been

---

intentional. But he will porcelain to the whole world that he was insulted. Imagining that he has been the target of insults at all the events, he makes himself prone to mental strain and stress.

Not only this but when he is praised in a public function, it is taken as an insult by the others. Besides, when he is forced to take up an object or a project he considers distasteful, it seems to be a deliberate attempt at denigration. The act of ridiculing a person is also considered an insult.

How does one get rid of this, and how does one ignore it? You must find out who is the one whose status is the lowest among them when two different persons or more people meet. The respect and accolades he receives are the respect and accolades you can expect for yourself when you compare his status with yours. And when you have made peace with yourself in this way, then neither an insulting word or deed will affect you. The other thing is the person who is insulting you cannot ever be straightforward or dignified in his utterances. But the audience will judge him from different perspectives and its repercussions, if any, will be from many different angles.

Over Burdening

It is those who work sincerely and with respect for their work who are affected by overburdening. This happens in two ways. It is customary to overburden a person who has earned the reputation of being prompt and excellent at his work since it is believed he has the capacity to do it well even under pressure. The burden is placed on him with the firm belief that he alone can complete it gracefully. The other is overburdening a person with such work for which he has no skill, knowing his capacity and thus putting him under great mental stress.

In the first instance, the person benefits from the extra work thrust on him. But in the second one, the person is subject to mental stress because of a feeling of inadequacy that he is not able to do the work expected of him. Apart from these two, there are also those who take on extra burdens on themselves, in spite of knowing that they cannot do it, either for the love of money or to earn some fame and respect. However heavy the burden we have to carry what we need to reflect upon is why are we doing this? To earn money? To eat? Why do we eat? To maintain our bodies, of course. The question that arises now is, how much burden should one carry to maintain one's health. Do a simple calculation and bear the burden accordingly. That would be enough. It would ensure a healthy life for you. Instead, due to one's greed, we get ready to carry any amount of burden over a period of time, we find that we are not able to enjoy the money earned and instead go about finding ways and means to attain good health.

This is a completely wrong way of going about it. Be prepared is the motto to be adopted and learn to lead a stress-free life. Life itself should not become a burden. Your life's practices should help lighten the burden. The pleasure in life depends on how easily you perceive it. We face needless anxiety by worrying about how to face the future, how to meet our needs, and how to face challenges. Pause and look back. We will realize that over a period, we have faced the needs and challenges without even being aware of it and how the burden we thought was insurmountable has eased. Remember that the God who made us all, will come to the support of each one of us and help fulfill our needs at the right time. Days pass by. We age. But the burdens do not pile up. It is true that the burdens we face at various stages of life vanish at that stage itself.

Loss

Loss is an experience that happens to everyone suddenly but often. There are any number of losses such as loss of status. Losing out on various opportunities, loss of dear and near ones, and loss of lives and property due to natural calamities that we all have met in our lives. This could have resulted in mental stress too. The intensity of the mental stress changes with the severity of the loss. There is no life without loss.

Perspectives of Imperfection

Looking at the loss of status from this perspective, it can be said this is a loss that can be redeemed with tireless striving. It is the same with the loss of opportunities since opportunities keep cropping up every now and then. We should always prepare ourselves to make use of these opportunities. But the loss of our dear ones leads to stress. This loss could be due to natural calamities, death due to illnesses, or due to old age.

This has been happening since time immemorial for generations. All of us are subject to this, and it is a natural phenomenon. We have very short lives in this world. From the beginning to the end, we undergo such losses. In this short span of time, our aim should be to live our lives. We should not forget that all that we have is to lead a comfortable life and what we have beyond that is in excess of our wants.

If you consider that a loss, then we need to pause and ponder. We finally leave this mortal world without enjoying the wealth we have accumulated over the years of working. What is your loss in this situation? Nothing. It is a loss for your status. Having lost its owner, it is your status that will be in mourning. This is nature. If you start reflecting on such a situation, you will be forced to think of the objects and people for whom you have been at a loss. But do we worry about this? No, isn't it? Keeping this in mind, my request to all is not to get stressed by taking these losses to heart.

7

Ways to Face Depression

Most people in their journey of life would have faced a few of the above-discussed twelve different issues. Those who are not aware of the problems faced by others might think 'Why am I the only one to face such problems' and feel miserable. This is the wrong opinion. When they realize that the others are also on the same page, their misery is mitigated to a certain extent. Furthermore when they realize that the entire city or the whole nation is facing this issue, then even if the issue is a severe one, its effect on one's mental stress will appear much less. What is the reason for this? This is a form of comparison. That is a comparison of the problems. Will the stress become less just through comparison? Not at all. Just as the problems find a place in us and result in mental stress, there are a few ways, to use our mental strength to confront and overcome these problems. Generally, acceptance, countermeasures, changing directions, forgiving, sharing, fortitude or willpower, analyzing, prayer, forbearing, vacating (the place) are ten ways one has to learn and adopt in our lives.

How to face problems? For some, you can use ' acceptance ' as a weapon to rid yourself of it. For some, you have to use 'countermeasures' to find success. When you find some problems that do not concern you, then you should use your intelligence to 'change its direction'. In case you are confronted with some problems by mistake, then do not forget to use 'forgiveness' as a weapon against the person who attacked you. When it is confirmed that the entire problem is of your making, then 'accept' it and after a long and deep analysis from different perspectives, find a solution for it. When you are not able to find a solution for a problem and are confused, 'share' it, according to the problem with the right person, without delay. If you find that the problem arises out of the place around you, then it is better to 'vacate' the place. When you find that the problems cannot be shared with anyone then the best solution is to turn to God and pray to Him for an answer. Absolutely unexpected events and problems should be borne patiently with fortitude. It is imperative to find the willpower to confront and bear any problem that you may face. Let us look in detail into which weapons to use according to the the situation you find yourself in.

Acceptance

Not many can use 'Acceptance' as a tool. It may be an accusation, a praise, a criticism, a bonus, a victory, a defeat, a loss, or a punishment. Whatever it is, it makes one look at it from different angles before one can accept it. Why is this?

Acceptance{ **is a mind game**}depends on the mind. Struggles and losses are external. It is natural to find solutions for the external. The solution may be good or bad. The decision taken by the mind is called acceptance.

A great loss that happens naturally affects the mind in many different ways. This is true. It is natural. One should realize that this is part of nature. One has to accept that its impact will last a couple of days or months.

Let us examine with an example how much of a change should you undergo to make acceptance a part of your mindset. There is this house where a lot of importance is given to decor and beauty. The child drops a glass vase that was displayed as part of the decoration and breaks it. As parents, how will we react to this incident? The mind accepts it when the parents rush to the child and are relieved that the child is not hurt, without giving importance to the expensive broken vase. If the neighbor's child or the husband or the wife or the elderly had broken the glass vase instead of the little child, look at the level of acceptance now. We have seen different ways of handling situations in our daily lives. This does not merit a detailed description. You have to change your attitude and adapt yourself to the mindset of 'what has happened has happened' and that 'it is our child' kind of response. In this scenario, there is no scope for any kind of mental strain or stress.

The incident described above is an external one. The way the mind accepts the issues within it, with no external manifestation is slightly different. One has to develop the kind of mindset that tells you that what has happened is wrong. There are many people who refuse to accept, all their lives, that what they have done is wrong, just to protect the family prestige. They will keep looking for that elusive peace all their lives. Do not wait for its impact on others. Once you realize that the mistake is yours, there should be no delay on your part in accepting the blame. One should understand that when there is a delay in accepting, there is a delay in finding peace too. Not only that, the delay gives rise to newer problems. Hence there should be no delay in acceptance. Otherwise, it will impact your health along with your mind.

It is normal for some confusion while accepting the external problems and their impact. Under the circumstances, we just nod our heads and temporarily exit from them. But the struggle goes on in the mind. It is better to calmly and patiently decide whether or not to accept them.

Acceptance doesn't stop with just problems. It happens even when you receive something as a gift or appreciation from someone. Should this be accepted or not? There is a slight hesitation here. The mind will explore these incidents. And when the mind starts calculating the possible repercussions, it is then that one is confused. The acceptance depends on knowing the character of the person who is the giver here.

In some instances, some people take the blame on themselves for doing good to others. They suffer the consequences of this action of theirs. This generally happens among a group of very close friends. Like helping in an emergency. This is a sacrifice. Such sacrifices are made to receive the blessings of God.

More than all these, it is very very important to accept one's faults and weaknesses. This will ensure that you receive God's forgiveness and lead a peaceful life. God does not give us directions or advice directly. If you can imbibe the advice given by parents, elders, and the wise, then lifelong advice can be avoided.

Let us practice acceptance in our lives and emerge victorious. It is certain that if we make acceptance a part and parcel of our lives, God will surely accept our prayers and help us lead a prosperous life.

Countermeasures

Events/incidents take place in our lives off and on. Some of these events are acceptable, but some are completely unacceptable. Accept the ones that your mind agrees with. At the same time, if you feel that you cannot accept those that are not appropriate for you but that they have been deliberately thrust on you with a view to taking revenge, it becomes essential to take countermeasures in such cases. Otherwise, such incidents will be imposed on you. Countermeasures are a way of provoking inner refusal and opposing objectively.

We know that our bodies have the capacity to fight diseases. There is a constant production of antibodies that do not allow the germs to grow. For example, chemical substances secreted by the skin, the acids secreted, and the fine hair in the nostrils help prevent illnesses. What happens when you sneeze because of dust or allergy? As a countermeasure, the air and with it the germs are expelled at high speed. Cells are battle-ready to destroy the microorganisms that attack our bodies. The body controls the duration and the intensity of the countermeasures. Just as the countermeasures organically take place to prevent illnesses at the physical level, so also we should adopt countermeasures to tackle the poison that acts on our minds externally. We should know how well to use these countermeasures. Being silent and calm is sometimes the best countermeasure. In some cases, it can be said that there is no better countermeasure than to project our victory in their presence. Such countermeasures can be exhibited through a peaceful demeanor and self-confidence.

Changing the Direction

When it is not possible to either accept or use countermeasures in some cases, then changing the direction is an excellent means to find a way out of the situation. This is done by taking a decision at the mental level without giving much importance to the problem but foregrounding the points that are in your favor and that are important for you, thus changing the direction, of the narrative to find a way out of the problem.

Towards this, you should equip yourself for introspection. There is a narrow path in a field. It is very narrow. Only one person can walk along it. Suppose there are two people coming from opposite directions. Both will start thinking.

Perspectives of Imperfection

Supposing both are bad people. Without giving way to the other each one wants the right of way, fights with each other, and in the end, with great difficulty squeezes their way through.

Suppose of the two, one is good and the other bad. The bad person will have his way and the good man will move out of the path and not wanting a confrontation find another path. So now there are two paths. If both are men of good intentions, they will each find a different path for themselves and leave the middle path unused, thus creating three paths. What we learn from this is that for two good men, the paths are three, for one good man and one bad man, there are two paths and for two bad men, there is only one path. Such incidents happen because of our thinking and through questions like, why and what for, by changing the direction.

This changing of directions should not be done openly in the presence of the opponent. It has to be done intelligently, without letting him be aware, that the direction has to be changed. Otherwise, this will only increase his hatred. In a family setting, when someone is asking for permission for an event and there is the possibility of danger and aftereffects because of this if you say no to the person, it could lead to the problem getting prolonged. Instead by clubbing it along with other related events and creating an amicable environment, you must change the direction. This will make them think.

Changing the direction does not mean dumping the problem on someone you don't like. They should be a part of the event. While changing directions, an important step to be followed is expectation. When the direction of a rain-bearing cloud changes, it moves to a different place but leaves a different weather pattern in that place. Instead of rain, there will be dryness. Sudden change. In the same way, after changing the direction of the problem, one has to wait calmly, and collect all the information about the concerned person to be ready in case the problem surfaces again.

Changing directions is a very important part of life. It becomes important to use this means to get relief from the problems that are likely to arise involving the family or the circle of friends. For instance, on a pleasure trip when the friends, being in high spirits, wish to swim in a dam in spite of knowing that it is dangerous, the majority say 'yes'. You can cite the presence of hidden crocodiles or some other incident and change the direction to escape from the problem temporarily. This decision may help in averting many a great calamity. Such changes are plenty in our lives. Let us think deeply and then act. Chase mental stress out of our way.

Forgiving

There is no escape from problems in life. Some can be accepted, some need countermeasures after acceptance, and for some the direction can be changed. While there is the need to adopt different measures to solve the problems, in some instances instead of looking at the means, there is a tendency to look at the person who is creating the problem and the reasons for the problem. In case the person is creating the problem due to ignorance, it is better to make inquiries, advise him, and forgive him. One has to take recourse to forgiveness when the solution to the problem is at the final stage. Only a person with patience is capable of making such decisions.

 Perspectives of Imperfection

Forgiving is the highest human quality. Forgiving can also be seen as an offering for bringing about changes in one's life. Though each person may give different explanations for it, forgiving, it can be said, has the ability to reduce the anger or the mental stress in us. Forgiveness acts as a tool to bring down the intensity of a person's anger. It also helps to progress in life instead of getting bogged down in further problems.

There is no one in this world who has not made mistakes. To argue that the mistake made is not a mistake but is the truth is the principle of those who are trying to attain perfection. Life lies in how one realizes that he has made a mistake. All of us who seek forgiveness from God must develop in ourselves the habit of forgiving others. The way we experience bliss when seeking forgiveness from God, in the same way when we forgive others we will experience release from the problems and lead a stress-free life.

For all those incidents that happen in families, whether sincere or likely to cause harm, if they are deserving of forgiveness, they should be forgiven and that is life. This does not mean that mistakes and harmful acts are to be accepted as part of life. Nor is it for using forgiveness at that moment and later continuing to make the same mistakes. Forgiving along with instilling the feeling of elation in us, the inclination to look for the good even in the worst of situations also leads us to a state where we can easily rid ourselves of mental stress. Forgiving has the quality to reduce the burden of guilt of any activity that is likely to cause harm to a person. It can free one from the clutches of those causing harm and at the same time make them understand the error of their ways. It brings peace into one's life. It fosters healthy relationships. It helps one to concentrate on one's life. It strengthens mental well-being. It helps develop a healthy heart and develops immunity to fight illnesses. One should not forget that forgiving benefits, not the one who forgives but the one who is forgiven. Since forgiving is a prerequisite for a healthy life, it becomes our duty to use it as a handy tool.

Sharing

Sharing is when the concept 'me' , 'mine' of selfishness is set aside. Sharing happens at various levels. It could be sharing of one's things, it could be sharing of ideas, it could be sharing of emotions, or sharing of confidences. This happens through friends, relatives, or through the media. Sharing broadens your mind. Its unique quality is that it generally encourages one's individuality. Sharing has the power to effect reconciliation among people and create confidence in the community.

The skills I have may not be enough to meet the needs of my life. In such a situation, in order to get what I need and in the public interest, sharing happens. Even the selfish ones, at some stage, enter the arena/ fortress of public interest through sharing. Selfishness is usually confined to the concept of perfection. Why does this shift from selfishness to public interest happen? What is the reason? And we should know at what stage does this happen?

By sharing your emotions and feelings you can come out of your selfish zone and find release from mental strain. Apart from finding release from selfishness it also results in enhancing the affection and regard from the society. The friends' circle widens.

People begin to understand you better. You get the opportunity to spend more time with people who have high regard for you. You can share not only your feelings but also your responsibilities. You can help create a stress-free environment if you openly share the problems at the workplace with a duly authorized and qualified person instead of suppressing them. There is nothing wrong in sharing the work allotted to you if you find it too much to handle on your own.

If you want to, you can successfully share your problems through some groups. Sharing need not be face-to-face. It can be done through cell phones or through different media. Sharing can also be one of the ways and means you adopt to find release from mental stress. You can share your desires too. Thus some of the events mentioned above can be shared with certain people and lead a peaceful life without stress.

Fortitude or Will Power

You should, first of all, develop the willpower to face the challenges that confront you. The struggles are always between people. Those who want to cheat you will deceive you by changing the narrative to suit their situation. Based on your willpower alone you will be able to make clear-cut decisions and at the same time convince others about them. If you are not able to instil such willpower then find out the reason for it. If you hide something you know and when things happen connected to it, then it will be difficult to gain the willpower needed to confront the situation. Though willpower depends on the mind, there are situations when both mind and body are involved. If you have the willpower you will surely find success. If one has to deliver a speech from a stage, the first thing he needs is willpower. It is only then that he can express his thoughts fully, clearly and lucidly.

At this stage, only if one has willpower can one face the world. It is wrong to depend on others' support for your willpower because their help may not be available when you need it. In such a situation your willpower gets weakened. Will power safeguards your physical health too. Otherwise, this will lead to unnecessary illnesses and suspicion. Progress in life is based entirely on your willpower and you are able to achieve your desired goal.

Your willpower should be used for good deeds. You should not use them for wicked deeds and be called obstinate and a wastrel. One should know when and for what one's willpower should be used. If and when you use your willpower for wrong things, then it puts paid to your progress in life. You will find that your willpower, when used for beneficial purposes, creates, at the final stage of success, willpower in you even without you being aware of it.

You must cultivate good qualities if you want to sustain your willpower. Otherwise, you feel discouraged when you face the opposite while exercising your willpower. You will not reap benefits if you use your willpower while following the wrong path. It is true that this will only increase your mental strain and stress. You may feel that your life is on an even keel but it is not true. Your willpower changes your attire, your attitude, and your habits.

The willpower manifests itself while facing the challenges the world poses. This willpower doesn't manifest itself in those who do not face challenges and it is age bound. It is when you are about to fail in your efforts that you will find that you need willpower and confidence to find success. It is your willpower that gives you the enthusiasm and urge to continue.

Analysing

The first thing to do when we are faced with any problem is to find out if the issue really concerns us. Do not accept it immediately. There are chances that in certain cases, the problem gets solved at the initial stage itself, thus escaping any mental stress. Once this stage is passed, one has to analyze the problem till one gets answers to questions like what is the reason for the problem, its origin, and who is the person behind the problem? There is, generally, a person hidden behind the problem.It may be a friend or an enemy. The problems that have a friend behind them need to be thoroughly analyzed rather than those from enemies. The reason could be that having moved closely and having gathered all the relevant information about us, they are likely to thrust the problem on us after making clear the problem. This would be as unbelievable as unexpected. When an enemy is involved, we have an instinctive awareness about it, and we will be careful. But when it is friends who are behind it, we have to deeply analyze the problem before arriving at a decision. The fear of misunderstanding a close friend and losing his friendship on one side and the anxiety at the involvement of a friend on the other would assail a person. In such a case, analyzing the problem will present a solution. Without analyzing one should not decide whether anything is good or evil.

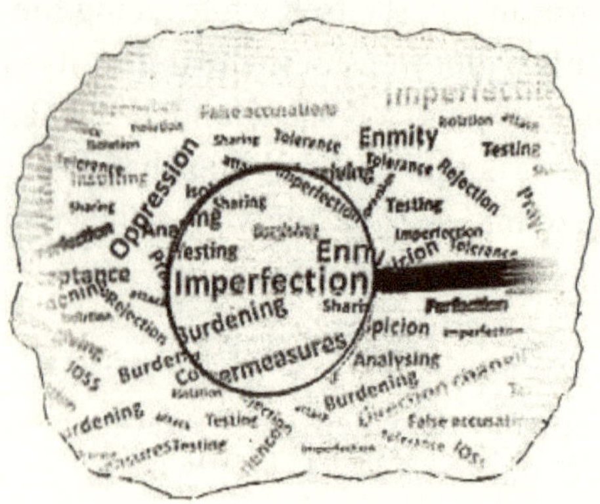

Before analysing some of the problems will be the appropriate time to analyse oneself. Only then, will you be able to find a way to deal with the problem. In the first place, it is best to use your brain to find a solution to the problem instead of leaving it to one's friends. When you are not able to find a solution, then it is best to turn to your friends. It is true that if you lose your temper when you are analyzing a problem, it will only compound the problem further. Hence patience and restraint are very important.

Prayer

When one faces events that throw up problems that are beyond one's capacity, that is when one needs prayers. When we are unable to find a way out and are in deep trouble or when we face trials and tribulations or when we want release from mental strain, the only solution is prayer to God for redemption.

When man has tried all possible measures in the world to find a solution to his problems, he establishes a relationship with God and finds relief. He communicates with God freely and frankly. He remembers God only when he has reached the end of human endeavor.

Praying is a tool used by all irrespective of the caste or religion he belongs to. Religion is based solely on prayers. Praying is as essential as breathing to life. We resort to prayers when all else like friends, relatives, kith, and kin, have given up on us and when the entire world looks at us with pity. This is a testing time for us. The pain then is unbearable. We are at our wit's end, not knowing what's to be done. The agony increases. We feel physically weak. The mind is in turmoil. Losses occur. Separations happen. Relationships collapse. Families face partitions within. You feel disgusted with the world. You detest yourself. Advice seems a nuisance.

Sometimes these testing times come as a blessing for those who use these trying times to understand life make necessary changes and reform oneself. Every failure, every struggle should be used by you to try and make yourself better. Fortify yourself mentally and be ready to fight to regain your lost health manifold. Success is yours. A person who overcomes such trials will not succumb to failures but will gain the admirable quality of tolerance. Not only that, they become living examples and role models for millions of others. A person who has withstood such testing times will undertake any task after due deliberation. He will start using prayers before problems strike and will find success.

Tolerance and Patience

Suffering and grief are inevitable for all human beings. Patience is the tool we need to overcome our anger when someone makes fun of us, causes us harm, or annoys us through their loose talk. For the ending to turn into an unpleasant one, intolerance should not be a reason. Those who are patient are sure to be the winners/rulers of the world. Patience is the virtue of the wise and the victorious, says the Tamil proverb. We are sure to find that even the hardest of tasks seem light if one has patience and tolerance. If we lose patience even our near and dear ones are likely to feel disgruntled with us. We should develop the maturity of mind to be able to tolerate the consequences and problems arising out of various events, even if for a short time only.

How much to tolerate is a question that everyone will ask. One should learn to be patient for a short while to be able to reap rich benefits. The patient waiting period is different for different events. Waiting for a longer period is not for greater benefits as this will have a detrimental effect on your health. When we use the internet and websites we expect faster results and hence less waiting period for your patience.

Patience is always beneficial and never otherwise. Hence it is advisable for people of all ages to be patient and tolerant. All good characteristics/qualities have patience as their basic feature.

　　　　Perspectives of Imperfection

Society has no use for those who are impatient and intolerant. The reason is that his other qualities such as anger, confusion, proud behavior, arrogance, and jealousy will surely lead to his downfall. Only those who have experienced it will appreciate the singularity of the virtue of patience.

An unplanned activity and impatient involvement will not be successful. You have to be patient at each and every event in your life. Patience is very important for all achievements and even scientific research. The patient wife of an unlettered man will bring up a responsible family. A sculpture is an embodiment of patience and deep reflection. What will happen if the sculptor loses his patience and capacity to reflect?

Hence, if you want to be an achiever in your life, you have to be a personification of patience. Let us adopt patience to face all challenges and systematically carry out whatever needs to be done and live successful lives.

Vacating / Escaping

When you are not able to stand alone and oppose a happening according to the situation or it is below your dignity to get involved in the problem then the only way out is to get out of the place which is what is referred to as ' vacating'. Tasting one grain of rice is enough to see if the rice is cooked is a Tamil proverb. Society judges you by the company you keep. Vacating is not like running away from a problem but a sensible way of avoiding certain situations that are likely to result in unnecessary mental stress and strain.

The decision to vacate the place should be taken on the basis of the nature of the problem, our connection with the problem, and what would be the immediate impact of the problem on us. Deliberately escaping or vacating from every situation is a sign of cowardice. This decision should be a well-thought-out one, without making an outward show of it. It should be based on a number of factors such as the problems discussed, who are all involved, what would be the next course of action, to which extent is the problem likely to proceed and the answers to these questions should decide whether to vacate the place or not. As a result, you will notice after a few days that the person responsible for the problem is not you but someone else.

That your decision was the right one should make you feel blessed.

Message from the Translator

"The first read of the manuscript of 'Perspectives of Imperfection' was refreshing. It was well thought out content wise, systematic in structure, its language rich and elegant. The task of translating it to English seemed challenging given all these parameters, but meeting this challenge proved an enriching experience".

This book delves deep into the various pressures we face in our daily lives, delineating in detail not only the pulls and pressures one faces at different stages in one's life but also in laying out in clear and simple terms the strategies to adopt, in meeting these pressures. This book will undoubtedly resonate with the readers as it skillfully navigates through various stages of life, the pressures one faces in each stage, from the members of the family, relatives, friends, the community and society as a whole.

This book is designed for all ages including the last when we get ready to face our Maker. It explores the past even as it evokes the present and envisions the future. I implore you to read on, share it with others and also benefit from it.

Let us live and let live.

Translated by

Rao Hemlatha S

Sunitha S Rao

www.ingramcontent.com/pod-product-compliance
Lightning Source LLC
Chambersburg PA
CBHW031425150726
47989CB00002B/801